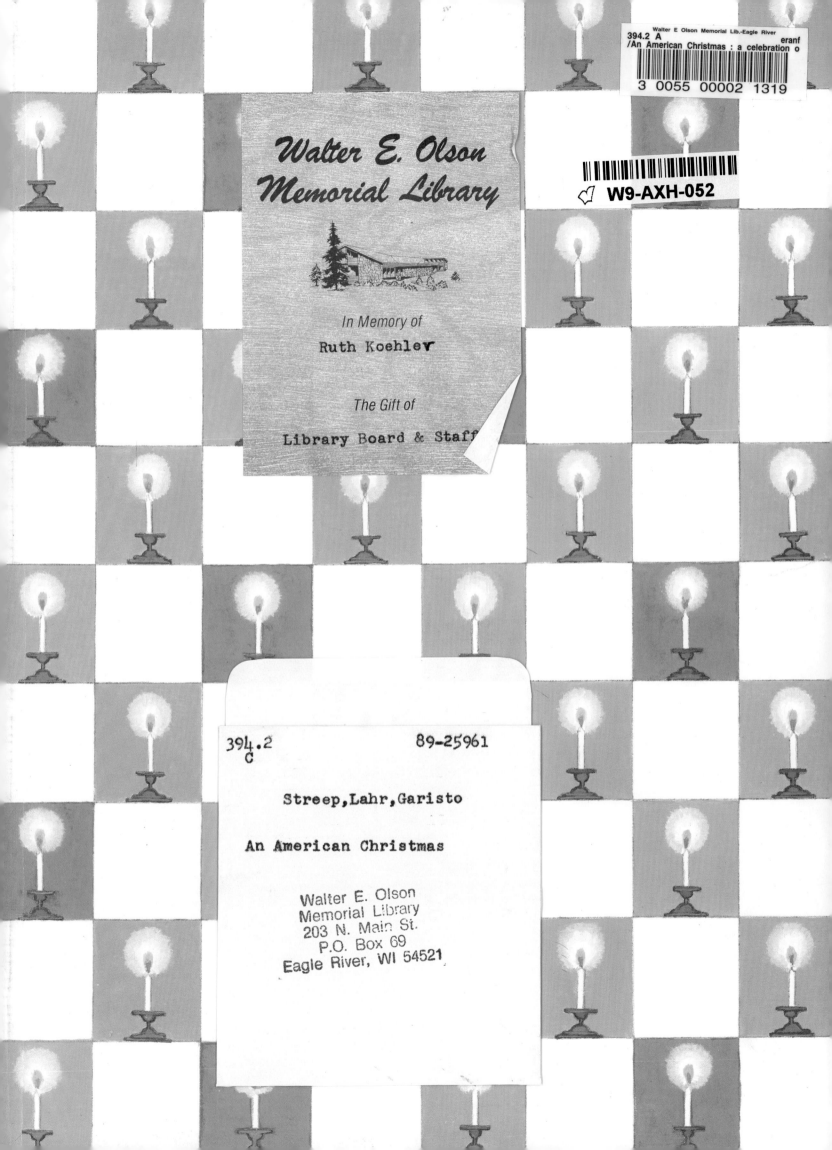

AN
AMERICAN
CHRISTMAS

AN AMERICAN CHRISTMAS

*A Celebration of Our Heritage
from Around the World*

Illustrated by
EMILY BOLAND

Edited by
PEG STREEP, JANE LAHR, AND
LESLIE GARISTO

PHILOSOPHICAL LIBRARY

NEW YORK

Library of Congress Cataloging-in-Publication Data

An American Christmas : a celebration of our
  heritage from around the world / illustrated by
  Emily Boland ; edited by Peg Streep, Jane Lahr,
  and Leslie Garisto.
         p.   cm.
     ISBN 0-8022-2570-5 : $39.95
     1. Christmas—United   States.   2. United
States—Social   life   and   customs.   3. Ethnic
folklore—United   States.   I. Boland,   Emily.
II. Streep, Peg.   III. Lahr, Jane.   IV. Garisto,
Leslie.
GT4986.A1A47   1989
394.2'68282'0973—dc20   89-8810
                                              CIP

Published 1989 by Allied Books Ltd., 31 West 21st
Street, New York, N.Y. 10010.
Illustrations copyright © Emily Boland, 1989.
Copyright © 1989 Jane Lahr Enterprises and
Promised Land Productions, Inc.
Printed in Spain by Cayfosa. Barcelona.

ACKNOWLEDGMENTS

We would like to thank the many consulates and friends who provided us with information and were willing to share their time and their recipes. Special thanks to Mrs. Karabaic and Mrs. Kestler, and to Bob Kestler for sharing his memories of a Hungarian-American Christmas.

"Angels from Heaven" and "Carol of the Hay" from *The International Book of Christmas Carols* by Walter Ehret and George K. Evans. Copyright © 1963, 1980 by Walter Ehret and George Evans. All rights reserved. Reprinted by permission of Viking Penguin, a division of Penguin Books U.S.A., Inc.

"Christmas at Hyde Park" and "Jesus Christ Is Born" originally appeared in *Christmas at Hyde Park* by Eleanor Roosevelt, published by Dodd, Mead & Company.

"The Gentle Beasts," translated by Leclaire Alger, originally appeared in *The Christmas Book of Legends and Stories* by Elva S. Smith and Alice Hazeltine, published by Lothrop, Lee and Shepard in 1912 and reissued in 1944.

"In Clean Hay" by Eric P. Kelly reprinted with permission of Macmillan Publishing Company. Copyright © 1932 by Macmillan Publishing Company, renewed 1960 by Katharine C. Kelly.

"Memories of Christmas" from *Quite Early One Morning* by Dylan Thomas. Copyright © 1954 by New Directions Publishing Corporation. Reprinted by permission of New Directions Publishing Corporation. U.S. Rights only. Canadian rights by permission of J. M. Dent and Sons, Ltd.

"The Miracle of the Fir Trees" by Jean Variot from *Happy Christmas* by Claire Huchet Bishop. Published by the Stephen Daye Press.

"Song from Heaven" by Hertha Pauli from *Tales of Christmas from Near and Far,* edited by Herbert Wernecke. Copyright © 1963 W.L. Jenkins. Used by permission of Westminster/John Knox Press.

"The Story of Bride" from *Christmastide Stories* by Vera E. Walker. Published by the National Sunday School Union, London.

"The Three Magi" by Pura Belpré from *The Animals' Christmas* , edited by Ann Thaxter Eaton. Copyright © 1944 by Ann Thaxter Eaton. Copyright renewed © 1971 by Jane E. Molitor, executrix of the Estate of Ann Thaxter Eaton. All rights reserved. Reprinted by permission of Viking Penguin, a division of Penguin Books U.S.A. Inc.

"The Three Skaters" courtesy of the Royal Netherlands Embassy, reprinted from *Santa Claus: The Dutch Way.*

"Which of the Nine?" by Maurus Jókai from *Christmas Stories from Many Lands,* edited by Herbert Wernecke. Copyright © 1963 W.L. Jenkins. Used by permission of Westminster/John Knox Press.

The packagers of this book have endeavored to acknowledge all copyright holders of the textual material reproduced in this book. However, in view of the complexity of securing copyright information, should any text not be correctly attributed, then the packagers shall undertake to make any appropriate changes in future editions of this book.

CONTENTS

SCANDINAVIA

Ice and darkness and frozen fields—Scandinavia in winter. The glint of grain and a blaze of light—this, too, is Scandinavia, as the Christmas celebration pushes back the darkness and anticipates spring's abundance. Long before Scandinavia was Christianized in the ninth century, her inhabitants celebrated the winter solstice with song, dance, feasting, and fire. Indeed, nowhere else in Europe are the old pagan customs so apparent in the Christmas tradition as they are in Scandinavia. Even the name of the holiday reverberates with the memory of ancient ceremonies: the solstice festival in honor of the god Thor was called Iol, Iul, Jule, or Yule, and the name not only survived, it traveled across an expanse of ocean to be adopted by English-speaking peoples in Europe and America. Though the Christmas customs of Sweden, Denmark, and Norway differ from country to country, all share the Norse influence, and all mark the holiday with images of light and bounty—traditions carried to the New World as well by Scandinavian immigrants.

10

Sweden

Whether on the streets of Stockholm or among the wheat fields of Minnesota, the Swedish holiday season begins on December 13th with the feast of Santa Lucia, the "Queen of Light." There are public and private Lucias—young girls dressed in white, crowned with candles and lingonberry leaves, portraying the Sicilian saint blinded and martyred in the fourth century. In Swedish homes on both sides of the Atlantic, the role of Lucia is reserved for the eldest daughter, who awakens the family with trays of coffee and *lusse-kattes* ("Lucy Cats"), saffron-scented buns baked in the shape of a cat's head or an X (for the Greek *chi,* the first letter in Christ). Lucy cats are sometimes known as *dovelskatter* ("devil's cats"), reflecting the ancient superstition that the solstice brought out the demons. According to Ruth Cole Kainen, author of *America's Christmas Heritage,* Lucia made her long journey from Sicily to Sweden in the Middle Ages when, crowned with fire, she appeared in a vision to Swedish peasants during a terrible famine; her miraculous appearance was followed by the arrival of ships bearing grain, and she was soon enshrined as a symbol of hope and plenty. Like most Scandinavian Christmas traditions, the veneration of Lucia is tied to pre-Christian worship as well—in this case to the goddess Freya, who also appeared, with a halo of fire, during a time of great privation.

11

The imagery of plenty—and the memory of famine—color the Swedish holiday, from the sheaves of grain left out for the birds to the observance, unique to the Swedish Christmas Eve, of "dipping in the kettle." At twilight the family gathers in the kitchen around a large kettle, in which has been prepared a broth of sausages, pork, and corned beef. Each member of the family spears a small piece of bread with a fork and dips it in the broth, thus commemorating a famine during which the Swedes existed only on broth and bread.

This meager but symbolic first course opens the lavish Christmas dinner: Dipping is typically followed by rice porridge in which is hidden a single almond; the finder, if unmarried, is guaranteed a spouse in the coming year. Next comes *lutfisk,* sundried, lye-cured ling (a saltwater fish similar to cod) that has been part of the holiday meal in Sweden since at least the sixteenth century. This is generally accompanied by a sort of bechamel sauce, along with boiled potatoes, pork sausages, herring salad, and a variety of Christmas sweets.

The Christmas Eve festivities culminate in the lighting of the tree, a tradition dating back only to the late nineteenth century, but as beloved in Sweden now as in its native Germany. The Swedish tree is hung with gilded pine cones, papier-mâché apples, homemade caramels wrapped in colored paper, gnomes, birds, glass balls, cotton to approximate snow, and glitter to imitate frost, as well as paper flags from around the world, and of course, a multitude of lights. The most popular decorations, however, are the straw goats and pigs that were once sacred to Thor. Beneath the tree are the gifts brought by the *Jultomten,* Sweden's bearded and red-suited answer to Santa Claus, whose roots reach back to the days when each house was believed to be protected by its own *tomten,* or gnome. Today tales of the mischievous *tomte* are as traditional at Christmastime as the tree itself. The Christmas Eve ceremonies close with the *judgedance,* a circle dance around the tree that was once a part of solstice ceremonies (summer and winter) in ancient Scandinavia. The dance is accompanied by the somewhat whimsical words of the old song:

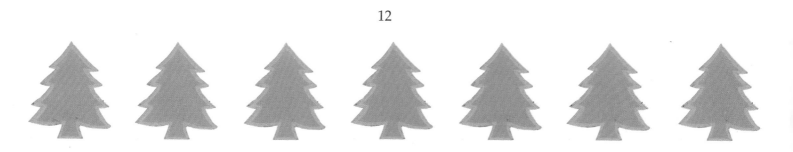

Now 'tis Yuletide again!
Yuletide will last, I think,
Till Easter.

No, this can't be so,
For between the two
Comes Lent.

Christmas itself is a quiet day in Sweden, reserved for churchgoing and kindling a fire against the darkness. At daybreak the Christmas candles are set out in every window, "to light the Christ child on his way." The churches, too, are awash with candlelight, from the altar to the nave.

The Christmas revelry resumes on December 26th, known to Swedes as Second Day Christmas, and continues until St. Knut's Day, January 13th. This is the day for putting out the candles, dismantling the tree, and repeating the old rhyme ("Twentieth Day Knut/Driveth Yule Out") that brings Christmas in Sweden to a happy—albeit reluctant—close.

Norway

Advent calendars may well have gotten their start in Norway; certainly, they mark the coming of the holiday as surely as the first snow presages the onset of the Norwegian winter. Norway may not deck herself out in pre-Christmas finery as Germany and England do, but Norwegians anticipate the holiday with fervor, hanging Advent calendars in their windows and setting out Advent candles—one for each Sunday of the season—in their churches and their homes. In many a home the Advent wreath—a gilded ring of candles—is suspended over the dining table in anticipation of Christmas.

As in Sweden, the predominant themes of the Norwegian holiday are fire and plenty. It is probably in Norway that the custom of the Christmas sheaf originated. Painstakingly preserved from the previous summer's harvest, the sheaves decorate office buildings and farmhouses alike, set out on poles and eaves and balconies to feed the birds and celebrate the promise of rebirth and regeneration.

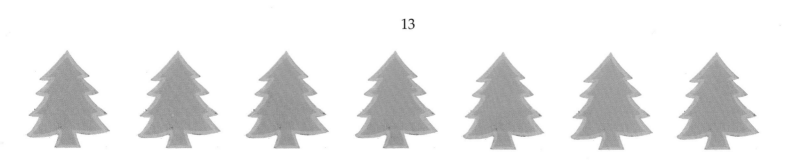

Feeding the hungry—and even the sated—is a holiday preoccupation in this land where famine is for most a distant memory. The preparation of food, often long in advance of the holiday, is so central to a Norwegian Christmas that the last Sunday in Advent is known as "Dirt Sunday," since no one celebrating Christmas with the right spirit could possibly have time for housecleaning. December 23rd, "Little Christmas Eve," is a night for getting together with family and sampling the festive dishes that have been many weeks in the making. No self-respecting cook serves fewer than seven of these, and almost always among them are the sugar and butter cookies known as *Berlinkranser.*

As in Sweden, the Christmas tree is a cherished, though comparatively recent, holiday tradition, and it is generally trimmed with paper chains, stars, and angels, and garlanded with Norwegian flags and electric lights—or, even today, real candles. In the afternoon, churches across the country celebrate the Children's Christmas, a service attended by and addressed to children, though adults are present as well. Few houses kindle a yule log, though the custom may well have originated here during the days of the Vikings, when it was believed to ward off evil spirits, abroad at the darkest time of the year. But a remnant of that ancient practice is the candle or electric light left burning in the window till dawn to give cheer and welcome to passing strangers.

By Epiphany the season is nearly spent; the Norwegians mark Twelfth Night with the dismantling of holiday decorations and a spare meal of boiled fish and potatoes. Still, one light remains unextinguished: a three-armed candle representing the Magi and their long midwinter journey.

Denmark

As Norway does, Denmark anticipates the holiday quietly, though all through December store windows bloom with marzipan fruits and flowers, and the heady smells of Christmas baking scent the air. Indeed, several weeks before Christmas comes Baking Day, when cooks the country over set up the dough for *brunekage,* the omnipresent molasses spice cookies that for many Danes are Christ-

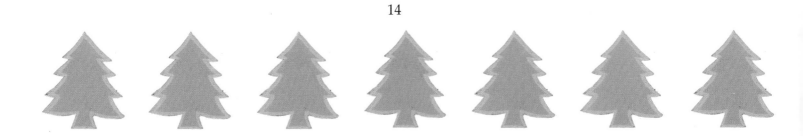

mas itself. Food is so central to the Danish holiday that tradition dictates every visitor must be well fed, lest he "bear the Yule spirit from the house."

There are other signs of Christmas as well: in December the *nisser* begin to appear, in store window displays and in the stories told to children about the Christmas gnomes who live in the lofts of old farmhouses. Like Sweden's *tomten,* the *nisser* were pagan household spirits who over time became associated with the holiday. On Christmas Eve, the story goes, they meet in the town church tower to help toll the bell in exchange for rice pudding, and in rural areas, a bowl of Christmas Eve pudding is still left for the resident *nisse* in the hayloft. The *nisser* are often joined in the store windows by the *julebukke*—straw billy goats that are a favorite holiday decoration and that harken back to the days of the Vikings, when the goat was sacred to Thor.

Like the Norwegian holiday, Christmas in Denmark begins in earnest on December 23rd, Little Christmas Eve, when family and friends gather to taste the sweets of the season—*fattigmand; klejner,* a deep-fried butter cookie; and, of course *brunekager.* As in Norway, Christmas Eve begins with the setting out of the *juleneg,* a sheaf of corn, usually hung in a tree, to feed the birds. The family celebrates with an early supper, whose first course is, predictably, rice pudding with its almond prize (in Denmark the finder receives neither good luck nor promise of a mate, but a piece of marzipan). Fruit-stuffed roast goose is the almost universal holiday meal, after which the tree—decorated with glazed-paper hearts and angels, and red and white Danish flags—is revealed. Presents are distributed, not by a *tomten* but by Santa Claus himself (or his familiar stand-in, the father of the house), and the family join hands and dance around the tree. Carols are sung, along with songs to Balder, the Norse sun god.

The Danish holiday draws to a close at Epiphany, with a ceremony that calls up the old images of hope and fertility: After the day's festivities have faded, young women as yet unwed walk backward to their beds, in order to dream of the men they will marry. The trees are down, the lights extinguished, but the midwinter dreams continue.

15

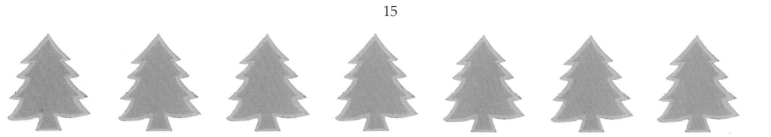

BERLINERKRANS

1   cup butter
½ cup sugar
2   hard-boiled egg yolks
2   uncooked egg yolks

3½ cups flour
2   egg whites
sugar for dipping

Soften butter and cream together butter and sugar. Mash the hardboiled egg yolks and add to butter mixture; add uncooked egg yolks and mix well. Gradually add flour until dough is firm but not sticky. Make individual rolls a little less than the thickness of a finger and about 4 to 4½ inches in length. Overlap the ends and dip them, first in the egg whites and then in the sugar. Bake on a lightly greased cookie sheet in a preheated 350-degree oven till lightly browned.

BRUNEKAGER

½ cup molasses, heated
¼ cup butter, melted
¼ cup brown sugar
¼ teaspoon each: ground cloves,
    nutmeg, ginger, cinnamon

½ teaspoon baking soda
dash salt
1   cup, plus 1 scant cup flour
sliced almonds for decoration

Mix together molasses, butter, brown sugar, spices, baking soda, and salt. Add flour little by little until well blended. Place the dough in a covered bowl and set it in a cool place for at least ten days (do not let it dry out). On baking day roll out the dough very thin, cut with cookie cutters (in Denmark the cookies are cut into the shapes of stars or diamonds), and place an almond in the center of each cookie. Bake about 5 minutes in a preheated 375-degree oven, till delicately browned.

MAKES ABOUT 100 COOKIES

RISGRYNSGRÖT
(SWEDISH RICE PORRIDGE)

2 cups rice
1 teaspoon salt
4 tablespoons butter

9 cups milk
1 stick cinnamon
1 almond

Cook the rice in three cups of salted water and 2 tablespoons of butter; gradually add the milk and cinnamon. Boil over low heat for an hour, and stir in remaining butter.

Before serving, drop in the almond. Serve with sugar, cinnamon, butter, and cold milk. It is said that whoever finds the almond will have good luck in the new year.

JULE KAKE
(NORWEGIAN CHRISTMAS BREAD)

2 cups milk, scalded
1 cup butter, melted
1 teaspoon salt
1 cup sugar
2 yeast cakes
2 egg yolks

8–9 cups flour
2 teaspoons cardamom
1/2 cup almonds, coarsely chopped
1 cup raisins
1/2 cup citron, chopped
1/2 cup candied cherries, chopped

Dissolve the yeast in 1/2 cup water. Add butter, salt, and sugar to the scalded milk. Let cool until lukewarm; then stir in yeast. Add egg yolks and 4 cups flour; let rise in a warm place until doubled. Punch down and add cardamom, nuts and fruits. Work in remaining flour until dough is elastic. Let rise again until doubled. Knead lightly, and place in two greased bread pans. Let rise for a third time. Bake at 350 degrees for 50 minutes. When cooled, the bread can be glazed with icing.

TRADITIONAL DANISH CAROL

Thy little ones, dear Lord, are we
And come Thy holy bed to see.
Enlighten every soul and mind
That we the way to Thee may find.

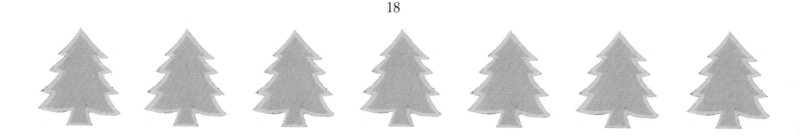

Julpepperkakor

The Swedish Christmas wouldn't be quite as festive without its *Julpepperkakor.* These lovely spice cookies are a Swedish turn on the familiar ginger snap.

1/3 cup water
1/3 cup dark corn syrup
3/4 cup light brown sugar
1/2 cup butter
1/4 teaspoon vanilla
1 1/2 teaspoons ground cinnamon

1 1/2 teaspoons ground ginger
1 teaspoon ground cloves
1 1/2 teaspoons baking soda
4 cups flour
1/4 teaspoon vanilla

In a medium-sized pot bring water, corn syrup, and sugar to a boil; add butter and stir until completely melted. Chill the mixture.

Add spices and baking soda mixed with a small amount of flour. Gradually stir in all the flour until dough is quite soft. Cover and keep in the refrigerator overnight.

Roll the dough onto a baking board and work until smooth. Roll out dough thin, using a pastry cloth (or flour the board and the rolling pin). Cut out the individual cookies with Christmas cookie cutters. Place cookies on a greased cookie sheet and bake in a hot oven (400° F.) for eight to ten minutes.

Let cookies cool before removing.

Icing (Optional)

1/2 cup powdered sugar

1/2 cup egg whites

Beat the sugar and egg whites together until smooth. Force through a fine paper tube and decorate cookies as desired.

Swedish Red Cabbage

This dish is traditionally served with the Christmas ham.

1 large red cabbage, tough outer
  leaves removed
3–4 tablespoons butter or bacon fat
3 Granny Smith (or other tart)
  apples, cored and sliced

juice of 2 lemons
sugar (to taste)
salt (to taste)

Shred cabbage, discarding tough center. Melt the butter in a saucepan, and add the cabbage, apples, salt (if desired), and the juice of 1 1/2 lemons. Cover and cook for two hours over low heat, stirring occasionally. Add sugar and additional lemon juice to taste.

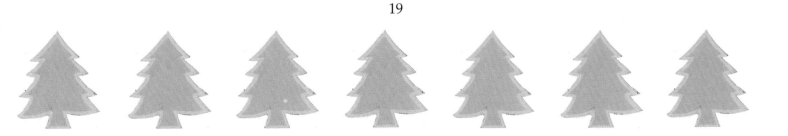

The Last Dream of the Old Oak Tree
A Christmas Tale

HANS CHRISTIAN ANDERSEN

In the forest, high up on the steep shore, hard by the open seacoast, stood a very old oak tree. It was exactly three hundred and sixty-five years old, but that long time was not more for the tree than just as many days would be to us men. We wake by day and sleep through the night, and then we have our dreams: it is different with the tree, which keeps awake through three seasons of the year, and does not get its sleep till winter comes. Winter is its time for rest, its night after the long day which is called spring, summer, and autumn.

On many a warm summer day the ephemera, the fly that lives but for a day, had danced around the tree's crown—had lived, enjoyed, and felt happy; and when the tiny creature rested for a moment in quiet bliss on one of the great fresh oak leaves, the tree always said:

"Poor little thing! Your whole life is but a single day! How very short! It's quite melancholy!"

"Melancholy! Why do you say that?" The ephemera would then always reply. "It is wonderfully bright, warm, and beautiful all around me, and that makes me rejoice!"

"But only one day, and then it's all done!"

"Done!" repeated the ephermera. "What's the meaning of 'done'? Are you 'done,' too?"

"No; I shall perhaps live for thousands of your days, and my day is whole seasons long! It's something so long, that you can't at all manage to reckon it out."

"No? Then I don't understand you. You say you have thousands of my days; but I have thousands of moments, in which I can be merry and happy. Does all the beauty of this world cease when you die?"

"No," replied the tree; "it will certainly last much longer—far longer than I can possibly think."

"Well, then, we have the same time, only that we reckon differently."

And the ephemera danced and floated in the air, and rejoiced in her delicate wings of gauze and velvet, and rejoiced in the balmy breezes laden with the fragrance of meadows and of wildroses and elder-flowers, of the garden hedges, wild thyme, and mint, and daisies; the scent of these was all so strong that the ephemera was almost intoxicated. The day was long and beautiful, full of joy and of sweet feeling, and when the sun sank low the little fly felt very agreeably tired from all its happiness and enjoyment. The delicate wings

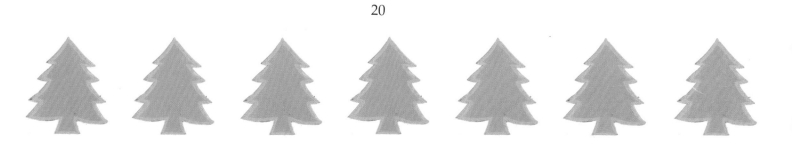

would not carry it any more, and quietly and slowly it glided down upon the soft grass blade, nodded its head as well as it could nod, and went quietly to sleep—and was dead.

"Poor little ephemera!" said the oak. "That was a terribly short life!"

And on every summer day the same dance was repeated, the same question and answer, and the same sleep. The same thing was repeated through whole generations of ephemera, and all of them felt equally merry and equally happy.

The oak stood there awake through the spring morning, the noon of summer, and the evening of autumn; and its time of rest, its night, was coming on apace. Winter was approaching.

Already the storms were singing their "good-night, good-night!" Here fell a leaf and there fell a leaf.

"We'll rock you, and dandle you! Go to sleep, go to sleep! We sing you to sleep, we shake you to sleep, but it does you good in your old twigs, does it not? They seem to crack for very joy! Sleep sweetly, sleep sweetly! It's your three hundred and sixty-fifth night. Properly speaking, you're only a stripling as yet! Sleep sweetly! The clouds strew down snow, there will be quite a coverlet, warm and protecting, around your feet. Sweet sleep to you, and pleasant dreams!"

And the oak tree stood there, denuded of all its leaves, to sleep through the long winter, and to dream many a dream, always about something that had happened to it—just as in the dreams of men.

The great oak had once been small—indeed, an acorn had been its cradle. According to human computation, it was now in its fourth century. It was the greatest and best tree in the forest; its crown towered far above all the other trees, and could be descried from afar across the sea, so that it served as a landmark to the sailors: the tree had no idea how many eyes were in the habit of seeking it. High up in its green summit the wood-pigeon built her nest, and the cuckoo sat in its boughs, and sang his song; and in autumn, when the leaves looked like thin plates of copper, the birds of passage came and rested there, before they flew away across the sea; but now it was winter, and the tree stood there leafless, so that every one could see how gnarled and crooked the branches were that shot forth from its trunk. Crows and rooks came and took their seat by turns in the boughs, and spoke of the hard times which were beginning, and of the difficulty of getting a living in winter.

It was just at the holy Christmas time when the tree dreamed its most glorious dream.

The tree had a distinct feeling of the festive time, and fancied he heard the bells ringing from the churches all around; and yet it seemed as if it were a fine summer's day, mild and warm. Fresh and green he spread out his mighty crown; the sunbeams played among

the twigs and the leaves; the air was full of the fragrance of herbs and blossoms; gay butterflies chased each other to and fro. The ephemeral insects danced as if all the world were created merely for them to dance and be merry in. All that the tree had experienced for years and years, and that had happened around him, seemed to pass by him again, as in a festive pageant. He saw the knights of ancient days ride by with their noble dames on gallant steeds, with plumes waving in their bonnets and falcons on their wrists. The huntinghorn sounded, and the dogs barked. He saw hostile warriors in colored jerkins and with shining weapons, with spear and halberd, pitching their tents and striking them again. The watchfires flames up anew, and men sang and slept under the branches of the tree. He saw loving couples meeting near his trunk, happily, in the moonshine; and they cut the initials of their names in the gray-green bark of his stem. Once—but long years had rolled by since then—citherns and aeolian harps had been hung up on his boughs by merry wanderers; and now they hung there again, and once again they sounded in tones of marvelous sweetness. The woodpigeons cooed, as if they were telling what the tree felt in all this, and the cuckoo called out to tell him how many summer days he had yet to live.

Then it appeared to him as if new life were rippling down into the remotest fibre of his root, and mounting up into his highest branches, to the tops of the leaves. The tree felt that he was stretching and spreading himself, and through his root he felt that there was life and motion even in the ground itself. He felt his strength increase, he grew higher, his stem shot up unceasingly; he grew more and more and his crown became fuller, and spread out; and in proportion as the tree grew, he felt his happiness increase, and his joyous hope that he should reach even higher—quite up to the warm brilliant sun.

Already he had grown high above the clouds, which floated past beneath his crown like dark troops of passage birds, or like great white swans. And every leaf of the tree had the gift of sight, as if it had eyes wherewith to see; the stars became visible in broad daylight, great and sparkling; each of them sparkled like a pair of eyes, mild and clear. They recalled to his memory well-known gentle eyes, eyes of children, eyes of lovers who had met beneath his boughs.

It was a marvelous spectacle, and one full of happiness and joy! And yet amid all this happiness the tree felt a longing, a yearning desire that all the other trees of the wood beneath him, and all the bushes, and herbs, and flowers, might be able to rise with him, that they too might see this splendor, and experience this joy. The great majestic oak was not quite happy in his happiness, while they all, great and little, were not about him; and this feeling of

yearning trembled through his every twig, through his every leaf, warmly and fervently as through a human heart.

The tree waved his crown to and fro, as if he sought something in his silent longing, and he looked down. Then he felt the fragrance of thyme, and soon afterward the more powerful scent of honeysuckle and violets; and he fancied he heard the cuckoo answering him.

Yes, through the clouds the green summits of the forest came peering up, and under himself the oak saw the other trees, as they grew and raised themselves aloft. Bushes and herbs shot up high, and some tore themselves up bodily by the roots to rise the quicker. The birch was the quickest of all. Like a white streak of lightning, its slender stem shot upwards in a zigzag line, and the branches spread around it like green gauze and like banners; all the woodland natives, even to the brown-plumed rushes, grew up with the rest, and the birds came too, and sang; and on the grass blade that fluttered aloft like a long silken ribbon into the air, sat the grasshopper cleaning his wings with his leg; the May beetles hummed, and the bees murmured, and every bird sang in his appointed manner; all was song and sound of gladness up into the high heaven.

"But the little blue flower by the waterside, where is that?" said the oak, "and the purple bellflower and the daisy?"—for, you see, the old oak tree wanted to have them all about him.

"We are here—we are here!" was shouted and sung in reply.

"But the beautiful thyme of last summer—and in the last year there was certainly a place here covered with lilies of the valley—and the wild apple tree that blossomed so splendidly! And all the glory of the wood that came year by year—if that had only just been born, it might have been here now!"

"We are here, we are here!" replied voices still higher in the air. It seemed as if they had flown on before.

"Why, that is beautiful, indescribably beautiful!" exclaimed the old oak tree rejoicingly. "I have them all around me, great and small; not one has been forgotten! How can so much happiness be imagined? How can it be possible?"

"In heaven, in the better land, it can be imagined, and it is possible!" the reply sounded through the air.

And the old tree, who grew on and on, felt how his roots were tearing themselves free from the ground.

"That's right, that's better than all," said the tree. "Now no fetters hold me! I can fly up now, to the very highest, in glory and in light! And all my beloved ones are with me, great and small—all of them, all!"

That was the dream of the old oak tree; and while he dreamt thus, a mighty storm came rushing over land and sea—at the holy Christmastide. The sea rolled great billows

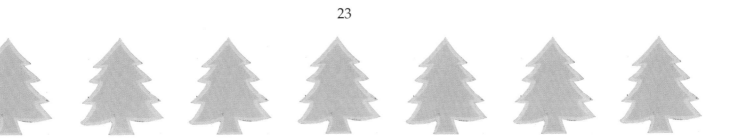

toward the shore; there was a cracking and crashing in the tree—his root was torn out of the ground in the very moment while he was dreaming that his root freed itself from the earth. He fell. His three hundred and sixty-five years were now as the single day of the ephemera.

On the morning of the Christmas festival, when the sun rose, the storm had subsided. From all the churches sounded the festive bells, and from every hearth, even from the smallest hut, arose the smoke in blue clouds, like the smoke from the altars of the druids of old at the feast of thanks-offerings. The sea became gradually calm, and on board a great ship in the offing, that had fought successfully with the tempest, all the flags were displayed, as a token of joy suitable to the festive day.

"The tree is down—the old oak tree, our landmark on the coast!" said the sailors. "It fell in the storm of last night. Who can replace it? No one can."

This was the funeral oration, short but well-meant, that was given to the tree, which lay stretched on the snowy covering on the seashore; and over its prostrate form sounded the notes of a song from the ship, a carol of the joys of Christmas, and of the redemption of the soul of man by His blood, and of eternal life.

Sing, sing aloud, this blessed morn—
It is fulfilled—and He is born:
Oh, joy without compare!
Hallelujah! Hallelujah!

Thus sounded the old psalm-tune, and every one on board the ship felt lifted up in his own way, through the song and the prayer, just as the old tree had felt lifted up in its last, its most beauteous dream in the Christmas night.

SPAIN

In Labastida, in the Spanish province of Alava, a lone shepherd stands in the quiet of a midwinter's night. He is joined by other shepherds, and the night's silence is punctuated with the cries of their flocks. Suddenly sound is everywhere: the tamp of boots on cobbled streets, the click of the shepherds' staffs beating out traditional dance rhythms, the delighted shouts of the children who've come to watch the parade. It is *la Noche Buena* ("the Good Night") in Spain, Christmas Eve, and in the words of a popular Spanish carol, *no es noche de dormir* ("it isn't a night for sleeping"). From the streets of Labastida the shepherds will make their way to the church for Midnight Mass, like so many of their countrymen from Madrid to Granada. Music, passion, drama, and devotion—these are the elements of a Spanish Christmas, and they are much the same whether the holiday is celebrated in Catalonia or California.

The start of the season is heralded to appear in early December by evergreens in the churches and outdoor Christmas markets. But the predominant harbinger of the season is the *nacimiento* or *belèn* (crèche), an Italian tradition wholeheartedly embraced by the Spanish. While each household has its own *nacimiento,* the most impressive are the life-size nativity scenes that decorate public places throughout Spain and, indeed, wherever people of Spanish descent celebrate the holiday. In Santa Fe, New Mexico, one unusual

nacimiento depicts not the manger but St. Francis of Assisi, the originator of the crèche, surrounded by animals both figurative and living.

In much of the Spanish-speaking world, however, the holiday begins in earnest on Christmas Eve. As in other Catholic countries, it is a day where fast is followed by feast, and the most important event of all is Midnight Mass. It is also the time of *Los Pastores*, vastly popular mystery plays that represent the shepherds' adoration of the Christ Child, and that are themselves rooted in the medieval passion plays known as *Autos sacramentales*. The same *Pastores* celebrated (by real shepherds) in the church at Labastida are also reenacted in New Mexico's mission village of Trampas, and in Spanish communities in Florida, Texas, Colorado, Arizona, and California.

An integral part of the *Pastores* is the singing of the *villancicos*, sacred songs that had their beginnings in the fifteenth century and have come more and more to be associated with the celebration of Christmas. In America as well as in Spain, the *Misa de Navidad,* or Christmas Mass, is likely to begin with the words of the traditional *villancico:*

> *Vamos todos a Belèn*
> (Let us all go to Bethlehem)
> *Con amor y gozo,*
> (With love and joy,)
> *Adoremos al Señor*
> (Let us adore the Lord)
> *Nuestro Redentor.*
> (Our Redeemer.)

Music in all forms marks the Spanish holiday. In December, outdoor markets begin to sell the *zambombas,* tambourines, miniature guitars, and metal mortars that accompany the *villancicos.* And on Christmas Day, Spanish children go from door to door reciting and caroling for sweets or small toys. (Christmas Day is also the time to share the larder's bounty, as friends and neighbors exchange cakes and other holiday desserts.)

Light, too, plays an important part in the holiday celebration. Though the latitudes of Spain remove it from the light-deprived sphere of northern Europe, since pre-Christian times the winter solstice was greeted by the lighting of bonfires on hills and mountaintops. Over the years, this tradition merged with that of the small winter fires lit by shepherds in the fields to become the *luminarias,* bonfires whose flames illumine church walls and public squares, reminding the celebrants not only of the coming of spring but of Christ, the Light of the World. In the sixteenth century, Spanish missionaries brought the Catholic liturgy to the New World, and with it the custom of the *luminarias.* In 1524 Fraya Toribio de Montolinía described Christmas among Mexico's Christianized Indians: In festive dress, singing the sacred songs translated by Spanish padres, they danced among shadows cast by the flickering bonfires.

When the Christmas Eve *luminarias* fade, it is time for the Dawn Mass, known also as *la Misa de Gallo* ("the Mass of the Rooster"). Spanish legend has it that, since no human visitors attended Christ's birth, it was left to the animals to praise and protect him on that first night. While the ox and the ass warmed him with their breath, the rooster flew to the stabletop and proclaimed Christ's birth to a sleeping world. His cries of *Cristo nacio!* ("Christ is born!") were miraculously answered by another rooster, singing out *En Belen!* ("In Bethlehem!").

The Spanish Christmas season not only continues into Epiphany, it culminates with it. Epiphany is the time for gift-giving, and it is on the holiday's eve that the Three Wise Kings arrive to fill the children's shoes with presents. Epiphany is also a day for feasting on

traditional Christmas foods like almond soup, truffled turkey, roasted chestnuts, *turron* (a hard nougat candy), *mazapan* (elsewhere known as marzipan) and, especially, the *Roscon de Reyes* ("Kings' cake"), which, like the French *roi de la fête*, contains a small prize (*la mona*) believed to convey good luck.

But the most cherished Epiphany tradition, from the *calles* of Barcelona to the streets of New York's Spanish Harlem, is the cavalcade of the kings, a parade not just of the kings themselves, but of their animals as well. (Indeed, it may be the only time of year that the sight of a camel on New York streets doesn't raise an eyebrow.) Of course, in the spirit of a Spanish Christmas, the kings are accompanied in their procession by the festive strains of music: As the holiday was greeted in December, so is it joyfully ushered out in January.

OLD SPANISH CAROL

Shall I tell you who will come
to Bethlehem on Christmas Morn,
who will kneel them gently down
before the Lord, newborn?

One small fish from the river,
with scales of red, red gold,
one wild bee from the heather,
one gray lamb from the fold,
one ox from the high pasture,
one black bull from the herd,
one goatling from the far hills,
one white, white bird.

And many children—God gave them
grace,
bringing tall candles to light Mary's
face.

Shall I tell you who will come
to Bethlehem on Christmas Morn,
who will kneel them gently down
before the Lord, newborn?

THE THREE MAGI

BY PURA BELPRÉ

Llegan de noche con gran cantela
Cuando ninguno sus pasos vela
Y al dormitoria del niño van
Y al dormitorio del niño van.

Swiftly they come in the night
As every one sleeps
And no one their footsteps watches
Then to the children's bedroom they go
Then to the children's bedroom they go.

It was the fifth of January, the eve of the "Three Kings" day. The day when all Spanish children eagerly await their Christmas presents.

In the sumptuous Palace of the Orient, where the Magi Kings lived, reigned great excitement and confusion. The royal doorman had been busy all morning answering the bell as the couriers came from the four corners of the world, bringing the royal mail. Inside the palace, the Chamberlain's voice could be heard giving orders to his hundred servants.

"Open the windows," he shouted, and a hundred men glittering in uniforms decked with gold and silver, in which the initials "M.M." (Magi Messengers) stood out, ran from one side of the spacious hall to the other, and opened wide the royal windows, letting in the cool air.

Kerchoo! Kerchoo! sneezed the Chamberlain.

"Bring my highest powdered wig," he called.

Again the hundred servants darted on, getting in each other's way, stumbling over chairs and sofas, until finally a very tall and thin one was able to free himself from the rest and bring out an immense wig, which he placed on the Chamberlain's head.

In the Royal kitchen the noise rose like a thunderous wave. Like a captain before his army, and clad in white apron and high cap, the royal chef stood. With hands folded across his voluminous stomach, he gravely directed his men. They carried out his orders with dexterity and care.

At his signal eggs were broken and beaten to soft fluffy foam, flour kneaded and almonds and nuts grated to a fine powder. From the oven and frying pans rose the smell of sweetmeats and roasts. It was evident that in the Royal Kitchen of the Three Magi, the innumerable cooks were getting ready an immense repast for a long journey.

Outside the palace in the Royal stables, the stamping and neighing of the Royal horses could be heard for miles around. Lines and lines of coaches, covered with heavy blankets, could be seen down the hall.

"There comes Carlos again," whispered a dapple grey horse to

another.

"Stop your stamping, stop it this minute," called out Carlos as he opened the door.

In reply the horses raised their heads and neighed loudly.

"I know, I know," said Carlos, "but this is the eve of the 'Three Kings' day, and it's the camels the Magi want and not horses."

Slowly he opened the door and led the camels to the public square. Already people were gathered there, while the stable hands brought gallons of water, baskets of scented soaps and a great number of combs and brushes.

The Royal Camels were about to receive their bath and this was a ceremony always performed in public. First the water was poured reverently over their backs. Then the stable boys divided in groups of ten and armed with soap and brushes began the scrubbing. This finished, another group would begin the combing and smoothing of the hair. Decked then with red mantles and silver reins, the three choice stable boys Carlos, Juan and Pedro led them to the door of the Royal Palace. The three magnificent looking camels of the Three Magi were the happiest camels in the entire world, for it was the 5th of January and they were to carry on their backs the three most-wished-for-persons in the children's world—King Gaspar, King Melchor, and King Baltazar. But they were impatient as they stood there. Putting their three heads together they asked each other:

"Where are the Three Magi? Why do they keep us waiting?"

And well might they ask, for the Three Kings could hardly be seen at that time.

In the Grand Throne Room, behind a barricade of opened envelopes they sat laughing and nodding to each other, as they read and carefully put away millions of letters sent to them.

There were letters of all sizes and colors. Some of them were written on fine paper with gilt borders, others embellished with flowers and birds, written in clear and legible handwriting, but the majority of them, and these were the ones the Kings liked best, were written on scraps of paper, and full of dots of ink and many erasures. They all carried the same message—a plea for some particular toy and a promise to be a better boy or girl in the future.

At last, the last letter was read and carefully put away. Slowly the Three Magi rose from their beautiful thrones and left the room. The Royal doorman saw them coming and opened the door wide. Solemn in their approach, majestic in their bearing, handsomely garbed with precious stones and jewelry, and with their ermine coats about them, the Three Magi of the Orient appeared at the door ready to mount their camels.

"How beautiful and handsome

they are," said Carlos to the other stable boys as they held the camels for the Magi to mount.

Large parcels of food and pastries, jugs of water and innumerable baskets full of all kinds of toys were brought out and tied tightly on the camels' backs.

They were soon off while the servants waved and wished them good luck.

On and on they went.

As they entered the desert, night fell.

"Dark and sombre indeed is the night," said King Gaspar.

"Fear not," remarked King Melchor, "the star will soon appear to guide us, as it appears every year. The same star that led us twenty centuries ago to the stable at Bethlehem."

He had hardly finished talking when up above their heads appeared a strange star glittering in the dark.

"Here is the star," said King Melchor again.

"Seems to me," said King Baltazar, "that on our last journey the star always appeared much later; however I may have lost all sense of time."

They followed the course it led . . . On and on they went.

For hours they travelled.

Suddenly from behind a cloud a ray of light appeared and darkness gave way to daylight.

The sun came out and the strange star disappeared.

Slowly the Three Magi pulled up their reins.

"Alas," they exclaimed. "What is the meaning of this?"

To their great surprise after having ridden away in the night, they were standing at their very door— the door of their own castle.

"What can this mean?" said King Gaspar.

"It means," answered King Melchor, "that in the course of the evening we have come back to our starting point."

"But we followed the star," said King Baltazar in a doleful voice.

"That was no star," piped a small voice.

"Wh-who speaks?" called out King Baltazar—this time in an excited voice.

"Oh, only me," said a little black beetle coming out from one of the camel's ears.

"You!" cried King Melchor, "how do you know?" "Tell us, little black beetle, tell us all you know," said King Gaspar.

"The star," said the little beetle, trying to raise its voice loud enough for them to hear, "was just a number of fireflies in formation to imitate a star."

"What are we to do?" moaned King Melchor. "We will never reach Spain. For the first time the children will find their shoes empty. What are we to do?"

"Shush—" said the beetle. "Look!"

Towards them running so fast his thin legs scarcely touched the ground, was coming a little grey mouse.

"Raton Perez!" exclaimed the Kings.

Making a low bow, he said:

"Yes, Raton Perez—bearer of good news!"

"Speak then," said the Kings.

"My Kings," said Raton Perez, "it's all the fault of the horses. They are very jealous. While they discussed their plans with the fireflies, I chanced to be resting on a bundle of straw. Too late to follow you, I thought of a plan to undo the fireflies' work. What could be easier than to ask Father Time? It was as you know a question of time and only He could arrange it. To my great surprise, I found Father Time sound asleep over his great cloak. Not to cause him the least discomfort, lest I should awaken him, I set his clock twenty-four hours back. So now my good Magi, ride on! The children of Spain must have their toys."

As if led by an invisible hand, the three camels pricked up their ears, raised their heads and went on towards the desert. Silence descended upon the group again. Above them the blue sky and all around them the sand, hot like fire under the rays of the sun. The Magi looked at each other in silence and set their eyes on the road.

Darkness soon closed in. On and on the camels went. They could hardly see themselves in the darkness that enveloped them.

Suddenly a star appeared large and resplendent, way up in the sky. Its light shone like a silver thread on the sand. In great silence, the Three Magi raised their heads to the sky, and gazed long at the star. There was hope and faith in the three eager faces that now bent their heads to lead the camels on.

From somewhere a sound of bells was heard, faintly at first, then louder and louder.

"God be praised," said King Baltazar, "we are near the city. It's the tolling of the bells—the bells from the church tower, ringing as a reminder of the entrance at Bethlehem years ago, letting us know, as they always do, that we are close to the city gates.

Ding—Dong—Ding—Dong—

The bells chimed merrily now and the hour of twelve struck. The camels shook their heads making all their headgear tinkle. Strangely enough they picked up the tempo of the bells and almost in unison passed the opened gate into the city.

That morning under each bed, inside each shoe, beside baskets and boxes wrapped with straw and flowers the children found their gifts, unaware of the hardships the Three Magi had in keeping faith with them.

ENGLAND, IRELAND, AND WALES

The crackle of flames in the grate, and above it a mantel garlanded with laurel and holly; the air spiced with pine and orange and clove; a pudding steaming aromatically on the stove; and, outside, ruddy-cheeked carolers in a swirl of snow. Of all the traditions that enhance an American Christmas, none are more deeply entrenched—or more evocative of the season—than those imported from England. Whether we live in a snow-covered New England village or a California beach community, for most of us Christmas will always have a distinctly Dickensian flavor. It is to our English cousins that we owe many of our most cherished

Christmas traditions. The holly that decorates the American hearth, for example, was first used in Celtic ceremonies that were later Christianized. (Indeed, that most English of English carols, "The Holly and the Ivy," was originally sung at pagan festivals and was probably rewritten sometime in the fourteenth century.) The hanging of mistletoe is also of English origin, along with the notion that anyone standing beneath it is fair game for kissing (mistletoe having once been, so the story goes, part of a Druid fertility rite). Long after the Druids disappeared from the British Isles, it was whispered that the maid *not* kissed beneath the mistletoe would remain unmarried all the following year; the fortunate lass who *did* receive a kiss was awarded a berry, plucked from the mistletoe, to seal her good luck.

And what more festive image than a fire dancing in the hearth? For this, too, we can thank our English ancestors, who every year at Christmastime heaved in a massive oak root, or "clog," and set it ablaze to chase away the midwinter's dark. Later the yule clog was more likely to be a simple log, but in either case tradition held that it be lighted with a piece saved from the previous year, which practice—as expressed in the old rhyme—sanctified the house and kept it safe from evil spirits:

> *Part must be kept wherewith to tende*
> *The Christmas log next yeare,*
> *And where 'tis safely kept, the fiend*
> *Can do no mischief there.*

From the yule log sprang the custom of Christmas candles, representing for Christians both the star of Bethlehem and the Light of the World, but also carrying echoes of ancient solstice ceremonies—yet another affirmation of light in a season of darkness. In Ireland, even today, few houses are without a triangular Christmas candle, its shape symbolizing the Trinity (or, some say, the Holy Family). Decorated with holly or colored paper cut in fantastic shapes, the candles are large enough to last until Epiphany, and sit in the window to welcome errant travelers out of the cold of an Irish night.

The Victorian era gloried in the trappings of Christmas, bequeathing us not only its customs but a tintype-and-sugarplum image of the holiday that lives on in our literature and our imaginations. (It was Victoria's German-born husband, Albert, who introduced the Christmas tree to an instantly enamored England.) Though English monks exchanged ornamented texts and pictures at Christmas well before the nineteenth century, it was Henry Cole, founder of the Victoria and Albert Museum, who came up with the idea in 1843 of commercially produced cards. Published by Joseph Crandall, these were small visiting cards bearing the colored images of holly, flowers, mistletoe, and so on. Crandall sold only one thousand cards in his first year of production, but less than twenty years later the custom was already *de rigueur* throughout England.

Another Victorian favorite, only now making inroads into the American celebration, is the Christmas cracker. Made of cardboard and colored tissue paper, the cylindrical crackers derive their name from the sound they make when pulled open by eager holiday revelers. They were introduced in 1840 by an enterprising London baker named Tom Smith, who drew inspiration from the gaily wrapped bonbons he saw in Paris confectioneries. Smith not only put the explosive "crack" in crackers, he also came up with the idea of filling them with small prizes—toys, epigrams, and paper hats (worn around the holiday dinner table by those willing to abandon their dignity in the name of good cheer). Smith's firm is still merrily churning out crackers, and numbers among its loyal customers the British Royal Family.

After the crackers and Christmas dinner, the Victorians retired to the sitting room to indulge in the whispered telling of ghost stories, or "Christmas tales." The custom may seem odd to those of us raised on such steadfastly upbeat classics as "Rudolph the Red-Nosed Reindeer" and "Frosty the Snowman," but the ghostly Christmas tale had its roots in the long-held belief that the powers of darkness were helpless in the presence of the Christ child and so could be safely discussed at the time of His birth. (Irish lore has it, similarly, that Christmas Eve is a night of omens; throughout the night the crow sings to chase away demons.) Eagerly awaited were the special collections, or "Christmas Numbers," published annually at the holiday, the most popular of which were edited by Charles Dickens. Two famous literary works that were fashioned as Christmas tales are Thomas Hood's "Haunted House" and Samuel Taylor Coleridge's "Rime of the Ancient Mariner." But by far the best known and best loved of all the tales—on both sides of the Atlantic—is Dickens's own "A Christmas Carol," whose story of a miser redeemed on Christmas Day by three spririts has for most of us lost its "ghost story" connotations.

The English passion for storytelling and the dramatic had another outlet in mumming, an ancient holiday tradition dating back at least to the Middle Ages. Extravagantly costumed, mummers put on masques and plays, both religious and secular, the most popular of which depicted the struggle between St. George and the Dragon (and often incongruously featured Father Christmas as well). The plays didn't exactly hew to reality: One 1850 masque listed as its cast of characters ("which speak") "Old Father Christmas, Young Grimston, Baron of Beef, Plum-Pudding, Mince-Pie, and Wassail-Bowl." In America the practice lives on most notably in the wild Philadelphia Mummers' Parade, held on New Year's Day, but the dramatization of the Christmas story that takes place in countless churches, town squares, and school auditoriums across the land no doubt owes something to the English custom of mumming as well.

England's greatest contribution to the American Christmas, however, may be less literary than culinary. An abundance of

English foods grace the American holiday table, from roast goose festooned with currants to roast beef and Yorkshire pudding to that flaming symbol of English Christmases past and present, the plum pudding (decked, à la Dickens, with a sprig of holly). Certain elements of the British feast have all but faded into obscurity; both the peacock and the boar's head once stood as the crowning glory of the holiday supper, but the first was unseated by the turkey in the seventeenth century (exported across the Atlantic from America) and the second lives on largely in the many "boar's head" carols written to extol the glories of the feast. One medieval favorite has survived the passing of the centuries, however—though in a dramatically altered form. The following fourteenth-century recipe for mince pie makes it clear that mincemeat began literally as minced meat:

A pheasant, a hare, a capon, 2 partridges, 2 pigeons, and 2 rabbits; their meat separated from the bones, to be chopped into a fine hash; and the livers and hearts of all these animals, also 2 kidneys of sheep; add little meatballs of beef with eggs; add pickled mushrooms, salt, pepper, vinegar, and various spices, pour into it the broth in which the bones were cooked. Put all into a crust of good pastry and bake.

Later—perhaps for economy's sake—dried fruits took the place of pheasant and hare, and the pies were molded into oblong shapes to represent the manger. Predictably, however, the Puritans condemned the practice as idolatrous, and so gave us the familiar sweet, round mince pie of Christmases English and American.

Ireland has its own holiday sweet, a hard griddle cake, eaten on New Year's Day. The cake is smashed against the door and, according to legend, whoever gets the piece that touched the floor first is guaranteed a home and cake the following year. The Scots, too, have their New Year's cake—Scottish shortbread, baked round and flat and always broken with the fingers, to represent the bread broken at the Last Supper.

The most ancient element of the British feast is probably the wassail bowl, dating back to the grace-cup of the Greeks and

Romans. The name itself derives from the Saxon *was haile* ("to your health"), and the "lamb's wool" punch served up in the bowl—consisting of ale, spiced and sweetened, and crowned with roasted apples—is probably Saxon in origin as well. Lamb's wool sometimes included toasted bread and roasted crabs in addition to apples, though the modern version is a good deal less exotic.

And so we still joyfully sing of "going a-wassailing," and dream of a Dickensian Christmas, and in the words of the old Welsh madrigal, deck our halls with boughs of holly. It's no wonder that when the American writer Washington Irving wrote about the holiday, he chose to describe an English Christmas, hailing it as a celebration "according to ancient custom." Mr. Irving would be pleased to find that much of that custom still thrives on his native shores.

FROM *A CHRISTMAS CAROL*

BY CHARLES DICKENS

Once upon a time—of all the good days in the year, on Christmas Eve—old Scrooge sat busy in his counting house. It was cold, bleak, biting weather: foggy withal: and he could hear the people in the court outside go wheezing up and down, beating their hands upon their breasts, and stamping their feet upon the pavement-stones to warm them. The city clocks had only just gone three, but it was quite dark already: it had not been light all day: and candles were flaring in the windows of the neighboring offices, like ruddy smears upon the palpable brown air. The fog came pouring in at every chink and keyhole, and was so dense without, that although the court was of the narrowest, the houses opposite were mere phantoms. To see the dingy cloud come drooping down, obscuring everything, one might have thought that Nature lived hard by, and was brewing on a large scale.

The door of Scrooge's counting-house was open that he might keep his eye upon his clerk, who in a dismal little cell beyond, a sort of tank, was copying letters. Scrooge had a very small fire, but the clerk's fire was so very much smaller that it looked like one coal. But he couldn't replenish it, for Scrooge kept the coal-box in his own room; and so surely as the clerk came in with the shovel, the master predicted that it would be necessary for them to part. Wherefore the clerk put on his white comforter, and tried to warm himself at the candle; in which effort, not being a man of strong imagination, he failed.

"A merry Christmas, uncle! God save you!" cried a cheerful voice. It was the voice of Scrooge's nephew, who came upon him so quickly that this was the first intimation he had of his approach.

"Bah!" said Scrooge, "Humbug!"

He had so heated himself with rapid walking in the fog and frost, this nephew of Scrooge's that he was all in a glow; his face was ruddy and handsome; his eyes sparkled, and his breath smoked again.

"Christmas a humbug, uncle!" said Scrooge's nephew. "You don't mean that, I am sure?"

"I do," said Scrooge. "Merry Christmas! What right have you to be merry? What reason have you to be merry? You're poor enough."

"Come, then," returned the nephew gaily. "What right have you to be dismal? What reason have you to be morose? You're rich enough."

Scrooge having no better answer ready on the spur of the moment, said, "Bah!" again; and followed it up with "Humbug."

"Don't be cross, uncle," said the nephew.

"What else can I be," returned the uncle, "when I live in such a world of fools as this? Merry Christmas! Out upon merry Christmas! What's Christmas time to you but a time for paying bills without money; a time for finding yourself a year older, and not an hour richer; a time for balancing your books and having every item in 'em through a round dozen of months presented dead against you? If I could work my will," said Scrooge, indignantly, "every idiot who goes about with 'Merry Christmas,' on his lips should be boiled with his own pudding, and buried with a stake of holly through his heart. He should!"

"Uncle!" pleaded the nephew.

"Nephew!" returned the uncle, sternly, "Keep Christmas in your own way, and let me keep it in mine."

"Keep it!" repeated Scrooge's nephew. "But you don't keep it."

"Let me leave it alone, then," said Scrooge. "Much good may it do you! Much good it has ever done you!"

"There are many things from which I might have derived good, by which I have not profited, I dare say," returned the nephew, "Christmas among the rest. But I am sure I have always thought of Christmas time, when it has come round—apart from the veneration due to its sacred name and origin, if anything belonging to it can be apart from that—as a good time: a kind, forgiving, charitable, pleasant time: the only time I know of, in the long calendar of the year, when men and women seem by one consent to open their shut-up hearts freely, and to think of people below them as if they really were fellow-passengers to the grave, and not another race of creatures bound on other journeys. And therefore, uncle, though it has never put a scrap of gold or silver in my pocket, I believe that it *has* done me good, and *will* do me good; and I say, God bless it!"

I SAW THREE SHIPS
Traditional

As I sat on a sunny bank,
On Christmas Day in the morning.

I spied three ships come sailing by,
On Christmas Day in the morning.

And who should be with those three
*   ships*
But Joseph and his fair lady!

O he did whistle, and she did sing,
On Christmas Day in the morning.

And all the bells on earth did ring,
On Christmas Day in the morning.

For joy that our Savior He was born
On Christmas Day in the morning.

MISTLETOE
by Walter de la Mare

Sitting under the mistletoe
(Pale green, fairy mistletoe),
One last candle burning low,
All the sleepy dancers gone,
Just one candle burning on,
Shadows lurking everywhere:
Some one came, and kissed me there.

Tired I was; my head would go
Nodding under the mistletoe
(Pale green, fairy mistletoe),
No footsteps came, no voice, but only,
Just as I sat there, sleepy, lonely,
Stooped in the still and shadowy air
Lips unseen—and kissed me there.

CAROL OF THE FIELD MICE

from The Wind in the Willows
by Kenneth Grahame

Villagers all, this frosty tide,
Let your doors swing open wide,
Though wind may follow, and snow
beside,
Yet draw us in by your fire to bide;
Joy shall be yours in the morning!

Here we stand in the cold and the sleet,
Blowing fingers and stamping feet,
Come from far away you to greet—
you by the fire and we in the street—
Bidding you joy in the morning!

For ere one half of the night was gone,
Sudden a star has led us on,
Raining bliss and benison—
Bliss tomorrow and more anon,
Joy for every morning!

Goodman Joseph toiled through the
snow—
Saw the star o'er a stable low;
Mary she might not further go—
Welcome thatch, and litter below!
Joy was hers in the morning!

And then they heard the angels tell
"Who were the first to cry Nowell?
Animals all, as it befell,
In the stable where they did dwell!
Joy shall be theirs in the morning!"

THE HOLLY AND THE IVY

Traditional English Carol

The holly and the ivy,
When they are both full grown,
Of all the trees that are in the wood,
The holly bears the crown:

The rising of the sun
And the running of the deer,
The playing of the merry organ,
Sweet singing in the choir.

The holly bears a blossom,
As white as the lily flower,
And Mary bore sweet Jesus Christ,
To be our sweet Savior:

The holly bears a berry,
As red as any blood,
And Mary bore sweet Jesus Christ
To do poor sinners good:

The holly bears a prickle,
As sharp as any thorn,
And Mary bore sweet Jesus Christ
On Christmas day in the morn:

The holly bears a bark,
As bitter as any gall,
And Mary bore sweet Jesus Christ
For to redeem us all:

The holly and the ivy,
When they are both full grown,
Of all the trees that are in the wood,
The holly bears the crown.

A Christmas Carol

by Charles Dickens

I care not for spring; on his fickle wing
Let the blossoms and buds be borne:
He woos them amain with his
    treacherous rain,
And he scatters them ere the morn.
An inconstant elf, he knows not himself,
Nor his own changing mind an hour,
He'll smile in your face, and, with wry
    grimace,
He'll wither your youngest flower.

Let the summer sun to his bright home
    run,
He shall never be sought by me;
When he's dimmed by a cloud I can
    laugh aloud,
And care not how sulky he be!
For his darling child is the madness
    wild
That sports in fierce fever's train;
And when love is too strong, it don't
    last long,
As many have found to their pain.

A mild harvest night, by the tranquil
    light
Of the modest and gentle moon
Has a far sweeter sheen, for me, I wean
Than the broad and unblushing noon.
But every leaf awakens by grief,
As it lieth beneath the tree;
So let Autumn air be never so fair,
It by no means agrees with me.

But my song I troll out, for stout,
The hearty, the true, and the bold;
A bumper I drain, and with might and
    main
Give three cheers for this Christmas old!
We'll usher him in with a merry din
That shall gladden his joyous heart,
And we'll keep him up, while
    there's bite or sup,
And in fellowship good, we'll part.

In his fine honest pride, he scorns to hide
One jot of his hard-weather scars;
They're no disgrace, for there's much the
    same trace
On the cheeks of our bravest tars.
Then again I sing till the roof doth
    ring,
And it echoes from wall to wall
To the stout old wight, fair welcome to-
    night,
As the King of the Seasons all!

THE STORY OF BRIDE

BY VERA E. WALKER

Away in the green land of Ireland there lived a little girl whose name was Bride. Her hair was nearly as golden as the starry dandelions that grow in the grass; her eyes were as blue as the sea in summer; and her face was so kind and good that everyone who looked on her loved her. The children loved her, for she was gentle with them when she played, and she took care of the youngest and weakest. The grown-up people loved her because she was always ready to help them when they were in trouble or difficulty. If a cow had strayed away it was Bride who went after her, calling and calling till she found where the animal was and brought her back. When Bran the herd boy hurt his knee, it was Bride who knew where the herbs grew that would heal the sore place. Babies never cried when she held them, they always settled down in her arms as if she was their real mother and cooed themselves to sleep. And as for the cows and the lambs and all the other creatures, why they would follow her about anywhere, and they would stand still for as long as ever her hands would stroke them.

Now Bride lived in a tiny cottage with Dugall the herdsman, and looked after his house and milked his cows and spun wool for their clothing. Some sav that she was really a king's daughter and had been found by him when she was a tiny child.

As Bride went to her work every day, caring for the cows, and sweeping the cottage, preparing food or spinning at her wheel in the long evenings, her mind was full of dreams. Often and often she would picture to herself the land where our Lord Jesus lived. She thought of Him as He went about His daily work in the carpenter's shop, or as He put out His hands to heal the poor lepers and those that were blind and lame. Most of all she loved to dream of Him as He lay in the manger with His mother bending over Him, that first Christmas night.

One day she went down to the well to draw water for Dugall's horse, her rough blue cloak wrapped round her, her pitcher in her hand. Sitting down by the well she looked down into the clear cool water. Up on the rowan tree near by, a white bird sang marvellously, and as it sang Bride fell asleep, and as she

slept she dreamed.

In her dream she found herself in a little town in a far Eastern land, where the hot sun glared down on the flat-roofed white houses, and water was scarce indeed. She dreamed that she was the daughter of an innkeeper there, and that she had been left to care for the guests who came there. People had been coming all day and the little inn was full; there was not room for a single other guest, nor food for them to eat, nor water for them to drink. As Bride stood looking out into the darkening sky, she saw two travellers coming along the path that led to the inn. One was a tall grave man who walked with a staff, and the other a tired woman carrying a little babe in her arms. The travellers begged to be allowed to rest awhile and to drink some water. What was Bride to do? She went into the little courtyard of the inn and piled together the hay so that the mother might rest there.

"I have no water," she said sadly, as she put her own rough blue cloak round her. But the woman smiled at her so sweetly that Bride felt as if she must find something for her to drink. She went into the cowshed and there the cows gave her a little milk. She carried it carefully back to the courtyard. But when she reached it she started back in surprise. For there sat the mother holding the Babe in her arms and both shone with a great light and glory, and Bride knew who they were. She knelt down in front of the Babe and offered the milk. The woman took it and drank it, and then she rose very gently and laid the little Babe tenderly in Bride's arms. The man took Bride's cloak and put it round her again. And Bride was filled with such great happiness that she could neither speak nor move.

How she came back to Ireland she never knew—but suddenly she found herself sitting by the well again, with her pitcher of water, and the white bird still singing on the rowan tree overhead.

Presently some children came running towards her. "Bride, Bride!" They called, and then they said, "Oh, look at Bride's cloak!" For all the rough blue cloak that she wore was covered with shining starry jewels, and in the centre was a great star, just such a one as burned in the sky many hundred years ago, to tell men that the King of peace and goodwill was born.

And as for Bride, she took up her work again and her kind deeds and her gentle ways, wearing the cloak with the Star of the Christ child on it as a sign and a glory all her days.

MEMORIES OF CHRISTMAS
from *Quite Early One Morning*
BY DYLAN THOMAS

One Christmas was so much like another, in those years, around the sea town corner now, and out of all sound except the distant speaking of the voices I sometimes hear a moment before sleep, that I can never remember whether it snowed for six days and six nights when I was twelve or whether it snowed for twelve days and twelve nights when I was six; or whether the ice broke and the skating grocer vanished like a snowman through a white trap-door on that same Christmas Day that the mince-pies finished Uncle Arnold and we tobogganed down the seaward hill all the afternoon, on the best tea-tray, and Mrs. Griffiths complained, and we threw a snowball at her niece, and my hands burned so, with the heat and the cold when I held them in front of the fire, that I cried for twenty minutes and then had some jelly.

All the Christmases roll down the hill towards the Welsh-speaking sea like a snowball growing whiter and bigger and rounder, like a cold and headlong moon bundling down the sky that was our street; and they stop at the rim of the ice-edged, fish-freezing waves, and I plunge my hands in the snow and bring out whatever I can find; holly or robins or pudding, squabbles and carols and oranges and tin whistles, and the fire in the front room, and bang go the crackers, and holy, holy, holy, ring the bells, and the glass bells shaking on the tree, and Mother Goose, and Struwelpeter—oh! the baby-burning flames and the clacking scissorman!—Bill Bunter and *Black Beauty, Little Women* and boys who have three helpings, Alice and Mrs. Potter's badgers, penknives, teddy-bears—named after a Mr. Theodore Bear, their inventor, or father, who died recently in the United States—mouth-organs, tin-soldiers, and blancmange, and Auntie Bessie playing "Pop Goes the Weasel" and "Nuts in May" and "Oranges and Lemons" on the untuned piano in the parlor all through the thimble-hiding musical-chairing blind-man's-buffing party at the end of the never-to-be-forgotten day at the end of the unremembered year.

In goes my hand into that wool-white bell-tongued ball of holidays resting at the margin of the carol-singing sea, and out comes Mrs. Prothero and the firemen.

It was on the afternoon of the day of Christmas Eve, and I was in Mrs. Prothero's garden, waiting for cats, with her son Jim. It was snowing. It was always snowing at Christmas; December, in my memory, is white

as Lapland, though there were no reindeers. But there were cats. Patient, cold, and callous, our hands wrapped in socks, we waited to snowball the cats. Sleek and long as jaguars and terrible-whiskered, spitting and snarling they would slink and sidle over the white back-garden walls, and the lynx-eyed hunters, Jim and I, fur-capped and moccasined trappers from Hudson's Bay off Eversley Road, would hurl our deadly snowballs at the green of their eyes. The wise cats never appeared. We were so still, Eskimo-footed arctic marksmen in the muffling silence of the eternal snows—eternal, ever since Wednesday—that we never heard Mrs. Prothero's first cry from her igloo at the bottom of the garden. Or, if we heard it at all, it was, to us, like the far-off challenge of our enemy and prey, the neighbour's Polar Cat. But soon the voice grew louder. "Fire!" cried Mrs. Prothero, and she beat the dinner-gong. And we ran down the garden, with the snowballs in our arms, towards the house, and smoke, indeed, was pouring out of the dining-room, and the gong was bombilating, and Mrs. Prothero was announcing ruin like a town-crier in Pompeii. This was better than all the cats in Wales standing on the wall in a row. We bounded into the house, laden with snowballs, and stopped at the open door of the smoke-filled room. Something was burning all right; perhaps it was Mr. Prothero, who always slept there

after midday dinner with a newspaper over his face; but he was standing in the middle of the room, saying "A fine Christmas!" and smacking at the smoke with a slipper.

"Call the fire-brigade," cried Mrs. Prothero as she beat the gong.

"They won't be there," said Mr. Prothero, "It's Christmas."

There was no fire to be seen, only clouds of smoke and Mr. Prothero standing in the middle of them, waving his slipper as though he were conducting.

"Do something," he said.

And we threw all our snowballs in the smoke—I think we missed Mr. Prothero—and ran out of the house to the telephone-box.

"Let's call the police as well," Jim said.

"And the ambulance,"

"And Ernie Jenkins, he likes fires."

But we only called the fire-brigade, and soon the fire-engine came and three tall men in helmets brought a hose into the house and Mr. Prothero got out just in time before they turned it on. Nobody could have had a noisier Christmas standing in the wet and smoky room. Jim's aunt, Miss Prothero, came downstairs and peered in at them. Jim and I waited, very quietly, to hear what she would say to them. She said the right thing always. She looked at the three tall firemen in their shining helmets, standing among the smoke and cin-

ders and dissolving snowballs, and she said: "Would you like something to read?"

Now out of that bright white snowball of Christmas gone comes the stocking, the stocking of stockings, that hung at the foot of the bed with the arm of a golliwog dangling over the top and small bells ringing in the toes. There was a company, gallant and scarlet but never nice to taste though I always tried when very young, of belted and busbied and musketed lead soldiers so soon to lose their heads and legs in the wars on the kitchen table after the tea-things, the mince-pies, and the cakes that I helped to make by stoning the raisins and eating them, had been cleared away; and a bag of moist and many-colored jelly-babies and a folded flag and a false nose and a tram-conductor's cap and a machine that punched tickets and rang a bell; never a catapult; once, by a mistake that no one could explain, a little hatchet; and a rubber buffalo, or it may have been a horse, with a yellow head and haphazard legs; and a celluloid duck that made, when you pressed it, a most unducklike noise, a mewing moo that an ambitious cat might make who wishes to be a cow; and a painting-book in which I could make the grass, the trees, the sea, and the animals any color I pleased; and still the dazzling sky-blue sheep are grazing in the red field under a flight of rainbow-beaked and pea-green birds.

Christmas morning was always over before you could say Jack Frost. And look! suddenly the pudding was burning! Bang the gong and call the fire-brigade and the book-loving firemen! Someone found the silver three-penny-bit with a currant on it; and the someone was always Uncle Arnold. The motto in my cracker read:

Let's all have fun this Christmas Day,
Let's play and sing and shout hooray!

and the grown-ups turned their eyes towards the ceiling, and Auntie Bessie, who had already been frightened, twice, by a clockwork mouse, whimpered at the sideboard and had some elderberry wine. And someone put a glass bowl full of nuts on the littered table, and my uncle said, as he said once every year: "I've got a shoe-nut here. Fetch me a shoe-horn to open it, boy."

And dinner was ended.

And I remember that on the afternoon of Christmas Day when the others sat around the fire and told each other that this was nothing, no, nothing, to the great snow-bound and turkey-proud yule-log-crackling holly-berry-bedizined and kissing-under-the-mistletoe Christmas when they were children, I would go out, school-capped and gloved and mufflered, with my bright new boots squeaking, into the white world on the seaward hill, to call on Jim and Dan and Jack and to walk with them through the silent snowscape of our town.

We went padding through the streets, leaving huge deep footprints in the snow, on the hidden pavements.

"I bet people'll think there's been hippoes."

"What would you do if you saw a hippo coming down Terrace Road?"

"I'd go like this, bang! I'd throw him over the railings and roll him down the hill and then I'd tickle him under the ear and he'd wag his tail . . ."

"What would you do if you saw two hippoes. . . ?"

Iron-flanked and bellowing he-hippoes clanked and blundered and battered through the scudding snow towards us as we passed by Mr. Daniel's house.

"Let's post Mr. Daniel a snowball through his letter-box."

"Let's write things in the snow."

"Let's write 'Mr. Daniel looks like a spaniel' all over his lawn."

"Look," Jack said, "I'm eating snow-pie."

"What's it taste like?"

"Like snow-pie," Jack said.

Or we walked on the white shore.

"Can the fishes see it's snowing?"

"They think it's the sky falling down."

The silent one-clouded heavens drifted on to the sea.

"All the old dogs have gone."

Dogs of a hundred mingled makes yapped in the summer at the sea-rim and yelped at the trespassing mountains of the waves.

"I bet St. Bernards would like it now."

And we were snowblind travellers lost on the north hills, and the great dewlapped dogs, with brandy-flasks round their necks, ambled and shambled up to us, baying "Excelsior."

We returned home through the desolate poor sea-facing streets where only a few children fumbled with bare red fingers in the thick wheel-rutted snow and cat-called after us, their voices fading away, as we trudged uphill, into the cries of the dock-birds and the hooters of ships out in the white and whirling bay.

Bring out the tall tales now that we told by the fire as we roasted chestnuts and the gaslight bubbled low. Ghosts with their heads under their arms trailed their chains and said "whooo" like owls in the long nights when I dared not look over my shoulder; wild beasts lurked in the cubby-hole under the stairs where the gas-meter ticked. "Once upon a time," Jim said, "There were three boys, just like us, who got lost in the dark in the snow, near Bethesda Chapel, and this is what happened to them. . . ." It was the most dreadful happening I had ever heard.

And I remember that we went singing carols once, a night or two before Christmas Eve, when there wasn't the shaving of a moon to light the secret, white flying streets. At the end of a long road was a drive that led to a large house, and we

stumbled up the darkness of the drive that night, each one of us afraid, each one holding a stone in his hand in case, and all of us too brave to say a word. The wind made through the drive-trees noises as of old and unpleasant and maybe web-footed men wheezing in caves. We reached the black bulk of the house.

"What shall we give them?" Dan whispered.

" 'Hark the Herald'? 'Christmas Comes but Once a Year'?"

"No," Jack said: "We'll sing 'Good King Wenceslas.' I'll count three."

One, two, three, and we began to sing, our voices high and seemingly distant in the snow-felted darkness round the house that was occupied by nobody we knew. We stood close together, near the dark door.

Good King Wenceslas looked out
On the Feast of Stephen.

And then a small, dry voice, like the voice of someone who has not spoken for a long time, suddenly joined our singing: a small, dry voice from the other side of the door: a small, dry voice through the key-hole. And when we stopped running we were outside our house; the front room was lovely and bright; the gramophone was playing; we saw the red and white balloons hanging from the gas-bracket; uncles and aunts sat by the fire; I thought I smelt our supper being fried in the kitchen. Everything was good again, and Christmas shone through all the familiar town.

"Perhaps it was a ghost," Jim said.

"Perhaps it was trolls," Dan said, who was always reading.

"Let's go in and see if there's any jelly left," Jack said. And we did that.

GOOD KING WENCESLAS

Good King Wenceslas look'd out
On the Feast of Stephen.
When the snow lay round about,
Deep, and crisp, and even:
Brightly shone the moon that night,
Tho' the frost was cruel,
When a poor man came in sight,
Gath'ring winter fuel.

"Hither page, and stand by me,
If thou know'st, telling,
Yonder peasant, who is he?
Where, and what his dwelling?"
"Sire, he lives a good league hence,
Underneath the mountain;
Right against the forest fence,
By St. Agnes' fountain."

"Bring me flesh and bring me wine,
Bring me pine logs hither;
Thou and I will see him dine
When we bear them hither."
Page and monarch forth they went,
Forth they went together
Through the rude wind's wild lament
And the bitter weather.

WHAT CHILD IS THIS?
Traditional, Fifteenth Century

What Child is this, who laid to rest
On Mary's lap, is sleeping?
Whom angels greet with anthems sweet,
While shepherds watch are keeping?

Refrain:

> *This, this is Christ the King,*
> *Whom shepherds guard and angels*
> * sing:*
> *Haste, haste to bring Him laud,*
> *The Babe, the Son of Mary.*

Why lies He in such mean estate,
Where ox and ass are feeding?
Good Christians fear: for sinners here
The silent Word is pleading.

> *Refrain*

So bring him incense, gold, and myrrh,
Come peasant, king to own Him;
The King of Kings salvation brings;
Let loving hearts enthrone Him!

> *Refrain*

A Christmas Tree
BY CHARLES DICKENS

I have been looking on, this evening, at a merry company of children assembled round that pretty German toy, a Christmas tree. The tree was planted in the middle of a great round table, and towered high above their heads. It was brilliantly lighted by a multitude of little tapers and everywhere sparkled and glittered with bright objects. There were rosy-cheeked dolls, hiding behind the green leaves; there were real watches (with movable hands, at least, and an endless capacity of being wound up) dangling from innumerable twigs; there were French-polished tables, chairs, bedsteads, wardrobes, eight-day clocks, and various other articles of domestic furniture (wonderfully made, in tin, at Wolverhampton), perched among the boughs, as if in preparation for some fairy housekeeping; there were jolly, broad-faced little men, much more agreeable in appearance than many real men—and no wonder, for their heads came off, and showed them to be full of sugarplums; there were fiddles and drums; there were tambourines, books, workboxes, paint boxes, sweetmeat boxes, peep-show boxes, and all kinds of boxes; there were trinkets for the elder girls, far brighter than any grown-up gold and jewels . . . there were guns, swords and banners . . . pen wipers, smelling bottles . . . real fruit . . . imitation apples, pears and walnuts, crammed with surprises; in short, as a pretty child, before me, delightedly whispered to another pretty child, "There was everything and more."

Being now at home again, and alone, the only person in the house awake, my thoughts are drawn back, by a fascination which I do not care to resist, to my own childhood. I begin to consider, what do we all remember best upon the branches of the Christmas tree of our own young Christmas days, by which we climbed to real life?

Straight, in the middle of the room, cramped in the freedom of its growth by now encircling walls or soon-reached ceiling, a shadowy tree arises; and, looking up into the

dreamy brightness of its top—for I observe in this tree the singular property that it appears to grow downward toward the earth—I look into my youngest Christmas recollection . . .

I see a wonderful row of little lights rise smoothly out of the ground, before a vast green curtain. Now a bell rings—a magic bell, which still sounds in my ears unlike all other bells—and music plays, amid a buzz of voices, and a fragrant smell of orange peel. Anon, the magic bell commands the music to cease, and the great green curtain rolls itself up majestically, and The Play begins. . . . Out of this delight springs the toy theater—there it is, with its familiar proscenium, and ladies in feathers, in the boxes!—and all its attendant occupation with paste and glue, and gum, and water colors, in the getting up of the Miller and His Men. . . .

Vast is the crop of such fruit, shining on our Christmas tree; in blossom, almost at the very top; ripening all down the boughs!

Among the later toys and fancies hanging there—as idle often and less pure—be the images once associated with the sweet old Waits, the softened music in the night, ever unalterable! Encircled by the social thoughts of Christmastime, still let the benignant figure of my childhood stand unchanged! In every cheerful image and suggestion that the season brings, may the bright star that rested above the poor roof be the star of all the Christian world! A moment's pause, O vanishing tree, of which the lower branches are dark to me as yet, and let me look once more! I know there are blank spaces on thy branches, where eyes that I have loved have looked and smiled; from which they are departed. But far above, I see the raiser of the dead girl, and the widow's son; and God is good! If age be hiding for me in the unseen portion of thy downward growth, O may I, with a gray head, turn a child's heart to that figure yet, and a child's trustfulness and confidence!

Now, the tree is decorated with bright merriment, and song, and dance, and cheerfulness. And they are welcome. Innocent and welcome be they ever held, beneath the branches of the Christmas tree, which cast no gloomy shadow.

ANGLO-NORMAN CHRISTMAS SONG

By some accounts, this is the earliest existing carol, dating from the thirteenth century:

Lordings listen to our lay—
We have come from far away
  To seek Christmas;
In this mansion we are told
He his yearly feast doth hold:
  'Tis to day!
May joy come from God above,
To all those who Christmas love!

Lordings, I now tell you true,
Christmas bringeth unto you
  Only mirth;
His house he fills with many a dish
Of bread and meat and also fish,
  To grace the day.
May joy come from God above,
To all those who Christmas love.

Lordings, through our army's band
They say—who spends with open hand
  Free and fast,
And oft regales his many friends—
God gives him double what he spends,
To grace the day.
May joy come from God above,
To all those who Christmas love.

Lordings, wicked men eschew,
In them never shall you view
  Aught that's good;
Cowards are the rabble rout,
Kick and beat the grumblers out,
  To grace the day.
May joys come from God above,
To all those who Christmas love.

Lords, by Christmas and the host
Of this mansion hear my toast—
  Drink it well—
Each must drain his cup of wine,
And I the first will toss off mine:
  Thus I advise,
Here then I bid you all Wassail,
Cursed be he who will not say
  Drinkhail.

THE WASSAIL SONG
Traditional

Here we come a-wassailing
  Among the leaves so green,
Here we come a-wandering,
  So fair to be seen.
    Love and joy come to you,
    And to you your wassail too,
    And God bless you, and send
      you
    A happy new year.

We are not daily beggars
  That beg from door to door,
But we are neighbours' children
  Whom you have seen before.
    Love and joy come to you,
    And to you your wassail too,
    And God bless you, and send
      you
    A happy new year.

Good Master and good Mistress,
  As you sit by the fire,
Pray think of us poor children
  Who are wandering in the mire.
    Love and joy come to you,
    And to you your wassail too,
    And God bless you, and send
      you
    A happy new year.

We have a little purse
  Made of ratching leather skin;
We want some of your small change
  To line it well within.
    Love and joy come to you,
    And to you your wassail too,
    And God bless you, and send
      you
    A happy new year.

HOLLY SONG
from *As You Like It*
William Shakespeare

Blow blow, thou winter winde,
Thou art not so unkinde,
  As man's ingratitude
Thy tooth is not so keene,
Because thou art not seene,
  Although thy breath be rude.
Heigh ho, sing heigh ho, unto the
  greene holly,
Most friendship, is fayning; most
    Loving, meere folly:
  Then heigh ho, the holly,
    This Life is most jolly.

Freize, freize, thou bitter skie
Thou dost not bight so nigh
  As benefitts forgot:
Though thou the waters warpe,
Thy sting is not so sharpe,
  As friend remembered not.
Heigh ho, sing heigh ho, unto the
  greene holly,
Most friendship, is fayning; most
    Loving, meere folly:
  Then heigh ho, the holly,
    This Life is most jolly.

RING OUT WILD BELLS
by Alfred Tennyson

Ring out wild bells to the wild sky,
  The flying cloud, the frosty light:
  The year is dying in the night:
Ring out, wild bells, and let him die.

Ring out the old, ring in the new,
  Ring, happy bells, across the snow:
  The year is going, let him go;
Ring out the false, ring in the true.
  Ring out the grief that saps the
    mind,
  For those that here we see no more;
  Ring out the feud of rich and poor,
Ring in redress to all mankind.

Ring out the want, the care, the sin,
  The faithless coldness of the times;
  Ring out, ring out my mournful
    rhymes,
But ring the fuller minstrel in.

Ring out old shapes of foul disease,
  Ring out the narrowing lust of gold;
  Ring out the thousand wars of old,
Ring in the thousand years of peace.

Ring in the valiant man and free,
  The larger heart, the kindlier hand;
  Ring out the darkness of the land,
Ring in the Christ that is to be.

BEFORE THE PALING OF THE STARS

Christina G. Rossetti

Before the paling of the stars,
   Before the winter morn,
Before the earliest cockcrow,
   Jesus Christ was born:
Born in a stable,
   Cradled in a manger,
In the world His hands had made
   Born a stranger.

Priest and king lay fast asleep
   In Jerusalem,
Young and old lay fast asleep
   In crowded Bethlehem;
Saint and Angel, ox and ass,
   Kept a watch together
Before the Christmas daybreak
   In the winter weather.

Jesus on His mother's breast
   In the stable cold,
Spotless Lamb of God was He,
   Shepherd of the fold:
Let us kneel with Mary maid,
   With Joseph bent and hoary,
With Saint and Angel, ox and ass,
   To hail the King of Glory.

VOICES IN THE MIST

Alfred Tennyson

The time draws near the birth of
   Christ,
   The moon is hid, the night is still,
   The Christmas bells from hill to hill
Answer each other in the mist.

Four voices of four hamlets round,
   From far and near, on mead and
     moor,
   Swell out and fail, as if a door
Were shut before me and the sound:

Each voice four changes on the wind,
   That now dilate, and now decrease,
   Peace and goodwill, goodwill and
     peace,
Peace and goodwill, to all mankind.

OLD IRISH CAROL

God bless the master of this house,
   Likewise the mistress too.
May their barns be filled with wheat
   and corn,
   And their hearts be always true.

A merry Christmas is our wish
   Where'er we do appear,
To you a well-filled purse, a well-filled
   dish,
   And a happy bright New Year!

DECK THE HALLS
An Old Welsh Carol, Probably from the Sixteenth Century

Deck the halls with boughs of holly,
Fa la la la la la la la la
'Tis the season to be jolly
Fa la la la la la la la la
Don we now our gay apparel
Fa la la la la la la la la
Troll the ancient Yuletide carol
Fa la la la la la la la la

See the blazing Yule before us
Fa la la la la la la la la
Strike the harp and join the chorus
Fa la la la la la la la la
Follow me in merry measure
Fa la la la la la la la la
While I tell of Yuletide treasure
Fa la la la la la la la la

Fast a-way the old year passes
Fa la la la la la la la la
Hail the new, ye lads and lasses
Fa la la la la la la la la
Sing we joyous all together
Fa la la la la la la la la
Heedless of the wind and weather
Fa la la la la la la la la

GENTLE MEN
(from *The End of the Play*)
William Makepeace Thackeray

A gentleman, or old or young!
   (Bear kindly with my humble lays);
The sacred chorus first was sung
   Upon the first of Christmas days;
The shepherds heard it overhead—
   The joyful angels raised it then:
Glory to Heaven on high, *it said,*
   And peace on earth to gentle
      men.

My song, save this, is little worth;
   I lay the weary pen aside,
And wish you health, and love, and
      mirth,
   As fits the solemn Christmas-tide,
As fits the holy Christmas birth,
   Be this, good friends our carol still,
Be peace on earth, be peace on
      earth
To men of gentle will.

IRISH CHRISTMAS FRUIT CAKE

4 cups all-purpose flour, sifted
1 teaspoon allspice
1½ cups butter, softened
2 cups brown sugar
2 tablespoons molasses
6 eggs
1 cup cognac or fruit juice

¾ pound white seedless grapes
1 pound currants
4 ounces candied cherries
6 ounces candied citron
grated rind of 1 lemon
grated rind of one-half orange
½ cup chopped almonds

Preheat the oven to 325 degrees. Prepare either a 10 × 3 inch round pan or a 9 inch square pan by lining with brown paper and greasing lightly. In a medium bowl, sift flour and spice. Then, in a large bowl, cream butter, sugar, and molasses. Beat in the eggs, one egg at a time, alternating with a tablespoon of flour as you mix. Then mix the cognac or fruit juice with the remaining flour, add slowly to the egg and butter mixture. Blend fruits, rinds, and nuts well, and add to batter. Mix well.

Pour in the prepared pan. Cover the pan with a piece of greased brown paper, cut either into a circle or a square. Bake for 4½ hours or until a tester inserted into the center of the cake comes out clean.

Cool completely. Wrap airtight, and store up to two months in a cool, dry place.

This fruitcake may be iced (with confectioner's icing) or frosted (with almond paste), if desired.

SCOTTISH SHORTBREAD

½ cup butter, creamed
¼ cup granulated sugar

1 cup flour, sifted
lemon peel, minced

Add the sugar to the creamed butter slowly. Then work the sifted flour into the butter mixture until the dough is firm but sticky. Do not overmix. Form into a round ball, and press into a circle. Press lemon peel onto circle. Place onto a greased baking sheet and bake at 300 degrees for 30 minutes, until golden brown.

Traditionally, shortbread is not cut but broken. (Cutting it is said to bring bad luck.)

ROAST BEEF AND YORKSHIRE PUDDING

4 pound roast
2 large cloves garlic
¼ cup plus 2 tablespoons beef drippings

2 large eggs
1 cup milk
1 cup flour
salt

Meat should be at room temperature before roasting. Crack each piece of garlic and rub roast well, or cut garlic into small slivers and insert into slits in roast made with a sharp knife. Preheat oven to 550 degrees and place beef in roasting pan, fat side up, in the middle of the oven. Immediately lower oven temperature to 350 degrees and cook until meat thermometer reads 140 degrees (rare) to 170 degrees (well done). Let sit for 30 minutes before carving.

Meanwhile, increase oven temperature to 450 degrees, and pour ¼ cup of beef drippings into a 9 × 13″ rectangular ovenproof casserole. Prepare batter: Beat eggs until fluffy and add milk. Mix together flour and salt and blend into egg mixture. Add 2 tablespoons drippings and beat well. Pour into casserole and cook at 450 degrees for ten minutes, then reduce heat to 350 degrees and continue cooking until pudding puffs up and is lightly browned. Cut into squares and serve with the beef.

SERVES SIX.

PLUM PUDDING

1 cup raisins
1 cup currants
½ cup citron
1 cup pitted dried prunes
the grated rind of 1 lemon
the grated rind of 1 orange
1 cup chopped hazelnuts
1 teaspoon cinnamon
1 teaspoon freshly grated nutmeg
1 teaspoon ground cloves
½ teaspoon allspice
½ cup of brandy or rum
1 cup butter, softened
1 cup sugar
6 eggs, separated
2 cups fresh bread crumbs

Place the the fruit, nuts, rind, and spice in a large bowl, and add the liquor; stir occasionally and let stand overnight. Beat the butter and sugar until fluffy. In a separate bowl, beat the egg yolks until lemon-colored; then add to the sugar and butter mixture. Add the bread crumbs to the fruit and nuts, blending well; then add to the butter and egg mixture. Blend well. In a separate bowl, beat the egg whites until stiff and then fold into the pudding. Pour into two quart molds and steam for 4 hours.

SERVES 12

WASSAIL BOWL

An old Saxon custom, the wassail bowl was filled at Christmastime with "lamb's wool"—ale, sugar, spice, and roasted apples. Below, a recipe for wassail; feel free to vary the ingredients as you wish.

6 apples, either tart or crab apples
3 pints ale (room temperature)
1 cup brown sugar
1 teaspoon each of ground ginger,
cinnamon, and nutmeg
4 whole cloves
thin strips of lemon peel

Dry-roast the apples in moderate oven until they have almost burst. Combine one pint of the ale with the apples and other ingredients; simmer gently for 15 min- utes. Add the rest of the ale, and heat through.

SERVES SIX

Wine or sherry can also be added to this recipe.

NETHERLANDS

The Dutch December sky hangs gray and low; the canals and waterways freeze, and a foggy cold rain pelts the barren landscape. It's no wonder, then, that the warmth of the Dutch feast of *Sinterklaas* (or St. Nicholas, as he is known formally in other countries) on December 6th is eagerly awaited each winter.

Although *Sinterklaas* bears a vague resemblance to his American descendent Santa Claus, he is different in many ways. *Sinterklaas,* like the real St. Nicholas, is a bishop, dressed in a mitre and resplendent red robes; he arrives, amid great pomp and circumstance, from Spain each winter, accompanied by his Moorish servant Piet and his white steed to bring gifts and goodies to good children all over Holland. It has been said that the legend that he lives in Spain originated in the one-time power of the Spanish Empire. For centuries, all that surrounded Holland was indeed in Spanish hands.

St. Nicholas is the patron saint of merchants and

sailors, and since Holland was a nation of both, *Sinterklaas's* adoption by the Dutch was pehaps natural and inevitable. Yet it is the aspect of the real-life St. Nicholas' kindness toward children —the legends of how he saved lives and endowed penniless maidens—which lies at the heart of this Dutch holiday, which is first and foremost a holiday for children.

On December 5th, *Sinterklaas* Eve, Dutch children in years past carefully put their wooden shoes by a fireplace or window (intended to hold the gifts the good saint would leave them), as well as a bit of hay or carrot for his great white horse. Songs exhorting *Sinterklaas* were (and still are) sung, many of which bemoan the weather: "What if the bad weather keeps *Sinterklaas* away?" Of course, throughout these many centuries, neither the cold nor the wet has ever stopped him yet.

Gift-giving has a special flavor too, quite different from the traditions of other coun- tries. Each gift is carefully wrapped, some- times even disguised, so as to surprise the reci- pient; the present is usually accompanied by a poem or rhyme. The jocularity of the holiday is welcome during the bitter winter cold and formality of Dutch society throughout the year.

The *Sinterklaas* celebration has its own traditional confections, among them *speculaas, borstplaat,* and *letterbanket*.

As a Northern country, Holland has its share of old folk customs, in addition to *Sinterklaas,* which connect to the Christmas season. In centuries past, farmers would put away all their tools on Christmas Eve so that the ghost Derk and his boar would not trip as they roamed the countryside. If they did trip, it was said, the harvest in the coming year would fail. The idea of Derk clearly belongs to the larger Nordic tradition, which features similar ghosts and animals, among them Freyr and his pig. Weather was, in times past as now, important to the farmers of Holland, and the conditions on New Year's Eve were said to predict the weather for the coming new year. Clear skies boded well, as did a brisk north wind, while winds from the east and west brought naught but misery. Even now, in rural areas, customs are observed that have their roots in pre-Christian traditions: In Eastern Holland, the coming of Christ is anticipated by midwinter horn blowing which begins on the first Sunday of Advent and ends on Christmas Eve. The horns are fashioned from hollowed branches of the elder tree, and the eerie sound is answered from farm to farm.

Christmas Day—or rather the two days of Christmas, December 25th and December 26th, which the country celebrates—is not devoted to gift-giving but is a time for churchgoing and family gatherings and dinners. Roast hare, venison, goose, or turkey are most often the main dish served. Music is very much a part of the Dutch holiday, and recitals and concerts are given all over the country on the second Christmas day. Special drinks—such as Dutch eggnog *(advocaat)* and a mulled cocktail called *borenjongens—* are all part of the holiday festivities.

And even though *Sinterklaas* seems more dignified than our Santa Claus, it is good to remember that he too makes appearances at schools and stores, at parades and on television!

LETTERBANKET OR *KERSTKRANS*
(ALMOND PASTRY INITIAL OR CHRISTMAS WREATH)

On St. Nicholas Eve, this pastry is shaped into the initials of the family names; at Christmas, it is formed into a wreath shape.

½ cup sweet butter
1 cup sifted flour
¼ pound almonds, ground fine
½ cup sugar

1 egg, beaten
grated peel of 1 lemon
1 egg, beaten with a few drops of
*   water*

Cut butter into bits and, using fingers, mix into flour until the mix is the consistency of coarse meal. Add ice water one tablespoon at a time, mixing, until the dough begins to form into a ball, and wrap in wax paper. Chill for 30 minutes or longer.

Meanwhile, mix the ground almonds with sugar, egg, and grated peel. Roll onto a floured board and form several rolls one inch thick in diameter. Wrap in wax paper and chill.

Preheat the oven to 425 degrees. Roll out the dough into a shape approximately 3–4 inches wide and ⅛ of an inch thick. Place almond roll in center; fold dough over almond roll and seal ends with water. Shape into initial or wreath, as desired.

Place on floured baking sheet and brush with beaten egg (diluted with a few drops of water). Bake 30–35 minutes. The initial or wreath may be frosted with icing, or decorated with glazed cherries, if desired.

SEE THE MOON SHINE

See the moon shine through the trees,
Boys and girls, stop your play!
The wondrous eve is coming near,
St. Nicholas' Eve!
Our hearts pound with excitement—
Who'll get the cake? and who the rod?
Our hearts pound with excitement!

HEAR HOW THE WIND BLOWS . . .

Anyone who has been in Holland in the winter will appreciate why the weather plays a part in this traditional St. Nicholas song.

Hear how the wind blows through the
  trees,
It whistles within the house!
Will the good Saint come to visit
With the weather so foul?
Yes, he'll come in the dark of night,
Riding his fast-paced horse!
He'll surely come
If he knows we are waiting,
Yes, he'll surely come.
Yes, then, he'll surely come.
Listen, children: Who knocks at the
  door?
Listen, children: Who taps softly at the
  window?
Surely, it is a stranger,
Who is surely lost and cold.
Come, let us ask his name.
Saint Nicholas,
Saint Nicholas,
Come visit us tonight.
We've put straw and goodies in every
  corner.

THE THREE SKATERS

It was a cold and barren season. The year's harvest had been poor; the barns were only half filled. Farmers wondered how they would manage to pull through the winter, how to feed their hungry families and cattle, how to heat their homes. A tense stillness hung over the wide, cold Dutch land where heavy gray clouds almost touched the snowy fields. Along the canals. stretching straight and frozen till they faded away in the distance, the gnarled old willows stood in ragged rows like worried onlookers. A farmer skated home over the frozen canal. He had been to market that day, but all he had been able to get for his few pennies was a bagful of apples, which he carried over his shoulder. Hunching his back against the icy wind, he hurried along with steady strokes, thinking all the while how disappointed the family would be with the meager results of his marketing.

As he stopped for a moment to refasten his curved wooden skates, he thought he heard a soft, swishing sound in the distance. Peering through the falling dusk he recognized his neighbor, an elderly miller, who was carrying the few loaves of bread the baker had given him in exchange for his sack of flour. The two men greeted each other without a word as they skated on through the silent evening—each sunk in his own thoughts, each knowing that the other man's thoughts were similar to his own.

They halted at a little drawbridge too low to pass under. Without taking off their skates, they stepped on land and crossed over to the other side of the bridge. Just as they found themselves back on the canal again, they were joined by another neighbor of theirs, a pig farmer, who carried a side of bacon for which he had found no buyer in town.

The three silent men hurried on, the strong, regular strokes of their skates the only sounds in the wide, wintry landscape. There should be a moon somewhere; at least, the heavy clouds looked strangely lit, as by an inner light. It was getting even colder now and the men huddled deeper into their woolen mufflers. The old miller lagged somewhat behind, to shift the sack from one shoulder to the other. As he did so, he noticed that the moon was appearing from behind the clouds. One cold, stark beam pointed straight down on an old barn across the snowcovered pasture on the left.

Suddenly a sound came from that lonely barn—a sound as from a baby, crying. "Hey!" the miller called to his companions. "Hey, there—stop! Come over here!" The other two braked to a halt and turned around slowly, annoyed at the old man. It was cold and late; time to be home.

"Listen", said the miller, pointing his finger to the barn. There was no mistake—they heard it too. There was a baby crying in that barn.

"But that barn's been empty for years, ever since the old man built himself a new one next to the house", said the farmer.

"He keeps his sheep there", said

71

the pig farmer, "but that's not bleating."

For a moment the three men looked at each other. Then they removed their skates and stepped on land to find out. As they approached the moonlit barn the crying became quieter, a mere whimper now, as a gentle woman's voice began softly to hum a little tune. The neighbors shook their heads, completely baffled. They hesitated just for a second—then the miller moved forward and opened the barn door. All three stepped inside.

They had to become accustomed to the darkness at first, away from the clear shaft of moonlight. But as their eyes adjusted to the dim glow of the lantern inside, they saw that their ears had not deceived them. As if by common impulse, all three took off their caps. A young woman they had never seen before sat on the cold barn floor. In her arms she held a newborn Baby which she rocked gently to and fro. Her coat was wrapped around the little Boy who was now sleeping peacefully. An older man was raking together some hay in a corner near where the sheep stood. Now the mother laid down her baby tenderly on that little heap of softness in the cold, rough barn.

"We come from far away," the old man began to explain, as if to answer unspoken questions, "and we still have far to go. When it was time for the wife to have the Baby, we looked for shelter and we are grateful that we could have this barn. But we can't stay long, for we have no food and no firewood. We shall have to move on tomorrow . . ."

The three men just stood there, unable to speak, turning their hands. Then, driven as by one force,

each lowered the sack from his shoulder and emptied it in front of the young mother. The apples, the bread and the bacon gleamed curiously in lantern light. Her eyes shone with such peace and quiet acceptance that they felt a strange sense of well-being that they couldn't understand. One by one they took a shy look at the dozing infant, then turned around and left, gently closing the door behind them.

The clouds had disappeared and the moon shone brightly over the snow covered fields. The men put on their caps; knotted their mufflers tightly around their necks; and swung the empty bags across their shoulders. Back at the canal they tied on their skates and started on the last stretch home, each thinking of the little scene they had just witnessed.

One–two, one–two went the skates over the frozen waterway. It was strange, but none seemed to feel worried about coming home empty-handed. They felt almost light-hearted in the cold, frosty night. Yet it was as if the sacks they carried were getting heavier and heavier—as if someone dropped a new stone in them with every stroke they made. By the time they reached the village and removed their skates, they were bent almost double under the loads they carried. They couldn't explain it, but somehow knew that it was good. At the church the three men parted. The farmer, the miller and the pig farmer each went his own way, home to the family. The last few steps seemed almost unbearable, so heavy a weight was loaded upon their shoulders. As each opened his back door and stepped inside, he dumped the sack on the floor and looked at the expectant faces around the fireplace with the blue and white tiles.

Loud cheers went up. "Father!" "It's Father!" "Father is home!" All the youngsters jumped up and began to tug at the strings of the bags—pushing each other, laughing, romping and dancing around as if this were a new kind of game.

Oh, the miracle of it all! When the bags were finally opened and turned out over the kitchen floors, an abundance of food rolled across the neatly scrubbed tiles. And there weren't merely everyday things. There was candy for the children, Dutch honey cake for the mothers, and tobacco for the fathers, as well. What happy feasts they had that evening in the three homes!

When all was quiet again, each of the three men sat by his fireplace, contentedly puffing his pipe. But in spirit they were far away; their thoughts hovered around a moonlit barn, around a simple little lanternlit scene, where a miracle had come to pass.

HUNGARY

Church bells, sleigh bells, the tiny bell that signals the coming of the Christ child—among Hungarians, Christmas is rung in to the glorious pealing of bells. At midnight on the first Sunday in Advent, the tolling begins, ringing out against the winter darkness the long-awaited message that another Christmas season has begun. The devout head to Midnight Mass while the children dream of the bountiful visitors to come, first St. Nicholas and then the Christ child Himself.

Though the celebration of St. Nicholas's feast day on December 6th came rather late to Hungary (probably at the beginning of the nineteenth century), the custom became so much a part of the Hungarian Christmas that it traveled across the Atlantic to be celebrated among American families of Hungarian descent. As always, St. Nicholas creeps in after midnight, dressed in his bishop's robes, to fill the shoes of good children with toys and sweets and to leave burned coal for the truly naughty (a rare occurrence, it should be said).

In the days before Christmas, Hungarian households are redolent with the smells of holiday baking. Rich pastries, filled or studded with poppy seeds and coated with honey, emerge from thousands of ovens, in America as in Budapest. There are the marvelous *dios beigli*, flaky pastries filled with sweetened walnuts, and *bobalka*, a yeast-based dumpling boiled in sugared milk and rolled in honeyed nuts or poppy seeds. *Szalon cukor*, a rich fudgelike candy, is especially favored by Hungarian children.

A sure signal that Christmas is coming are the Nativity plays performed in schools and churches, a deep-rooted custom that can be traced back at least to the eleventh century, when mystery plays

74

were a part of the Christmas liturgy. Later, religious leaders deemed the plays too worldly in nature and they were taken up by schools and independent religious societies. No doubt the elders were offended by the eccentric side of the plays, which began soberly enough but ended with a comedy in which the shepherds took on comic airs and fought among themselves.

Some Hungarians still celebrate Santa Lucia's Day, December 13th, though nowhere is the holiday as significant as in Sweden. Before the introduction of the Gregorian calendar, however, Santa Lucia's Day marked the winter solstice, and so was considered a time of great significance, especially in the Hungarian countryside. This was the day on which chickens could be charmed to lay plentifully throughout the year, and witches walked freely among the pious.

For most Hungarians, however, even in America, the real holiday is Christmas Eve, and the jewel of the Hungarian Christmas Eve is the tree. Not even the Germans, who invented the Christmas tree, hold it in such high esteem or decorate and light it with such glorious abandon. For several days before Christmas the children of the house are forbidden access to the room in which the tree has been installed. Then, at twilight on Christmas Eve comes the tinkling of a small bell—the signal that the Christ child (or, in some families, the Christmas Angel) has arrived. The doors are flung open, the tree revealed, and the gifts lying beneath its boughs happily plundered. This is followed by the singing of carols, notably "Silent Night" (another beloved German import) and the traditional *"Menybol Az Angyal"* ("Angels from Heaven").

For most Hungarians, Christmas Eve ends a day of fasting, which means a meatless supper, usually incorporating some kind of fish. The meal begins with honeyed pudding and buns in a poppy seed sauce, followed by cabbage soup and an array of accompaniments. Non-Catholics often serve stuffed cabbage in place of soup, and in most households the meal ends with a selection of Christmas pastries and mixed dried fruit.

The bells at midnight announce the first Christmas Mass, just as four weeks earlier they rang in the first Sunday in Advent. From now until late on Christmas night Hungarians will gather together in churches and around Christmas trees to sing the familiar words of the shepherds' carol: "Arise, ye shepherds, arise!/Glad tidings to you we bring:/Today a savior was born to us/In a manger in Bethlehem." And everywhere around them, as if in accompaniment, the church bells will toll out final greetings of the season.

ANGELS FROM HEAVEN
Traditional Hungarian Carol

Angels from heaven say to the shepherds,
"News we bring, News we bring!
In Bethlehem, asleep in a manger,
Lies your King, lies your King!

"Though born so lowly, yet He is holy,
God's own Son, God's own Son!
He comes to earth to ransom and save
    you
Ev'ry one, ev'ry one!"

DIOS BEIGLI

PASTRY

1 1/2 ounces yeast
1/4 cup lukewarm milk
1 pound flour

1/2 pound butter
pinch of salt
beaten yolk of 1 egg

Dissolve yeast in milk. Add other ingredients and mix until smooth, adding more milk if needed. Let the mixture stand for 3 hours in the refrigerator. Roll out into a thin rectangle; spread with walnut filling (below). Roll up rectangle lengthwise and brush with egg yolk. Bake on a greased cookie sheet in a preheated 375 degree oven for about 50 minutes to an hour; let cool and slice.

FILLING

1 pound walnuts, finely chopped
1/2 pound confectioner's sugar
2 ounces sultanas

1 teaspoon vanilla
milk

Mix together nuts, sugar, sultanas, and vanilla. Add boiling milk until mixture attains a creamy consistency; it should be spreadable but not wet. Spread over pastry.

ANISE SEED COOKIES

2 1/2 cups flour, sifted
1/2 teaspoon baking powder
1/8 teaspoon salt
1 cup granulated sugar

1 cup butter, softened
2 egg yolks
vanilla
anise seed

Sift together the flour, baking powder, salt, and sugar. Gradually add the butter, then mix in the egg yolks and vanilla. Chill overnight. On a floured pastry board roll out very thin and cut with Christmas cookie cutters. Decorate with anise seed and place on an ungreased cookie sheet. Bake in a preheated 400 degree oven 7 to 9 minutes.

WHICH OF THE NINE?

MAURUS JÓKAI

O nce upon a time in the city of Budapest there lived a poor shoemaker who simply couldn't make ends meet. Not because people had suddenly decided to give up wearing boots, nor because the city council had passed an ordinance directing that shoes be sold at half price, nor even because his work was not satisfactory. Indeed, the good man did such excellent work that his customers actually complained that they couldn't wear out anything he had once sewed together. He had plenty of customers who paid him promptly and well enough; not one of them had run away without settling his bill. And yet Cobbler John couldn't make both ends meet.

The reason was that the good Lord had blessed him all too plentifully with nine children, all of them as healthy as acorns.

Then, one day, as if Cobbler John hadn't already had trouble enough, his wife died. Cobbler John was left alone in this world with nine children. Two or three of them were going to school; one or two were being tutored; one had to be carried round; gruel had to be cooked for the next; another had to be fed, the next one dressed, yet another washed. And on top of all this, he had to earn a living for all of them. Verily, brethren, this was a big job—just try it, in case you doubt it!

When the shoes were made for them, nine had to be made all at once; when bread was sliced, nine slices had to be cut all at one time. When beds were made ready, the entire room between window and door became one single bed, full of little and big blond and brunet heads.

"Oh, my dear Lord God, how thou hast blessed me," the good artisan often sighed while even after midnight he still worked and hammered away at his lasts in order to feed the bodies of so many souls, stopping occasionally to chide now one, now another, tossing restlessly in a dream. Nine they were—a round number nine. But thanks be to the Lord, there was still no cause for complaint, because all nine were healthy, obedient, beautiful, and well-behaved, blessed with sound bodies and stomachs. And rather should there be nine pieces of bread than one bottle of medicine; rather nine side by side than coffins between them. But none of Cobbler John's children had the slightest intention of dying. It was already fated that all nine of them should fight their way through life and not yield their places to anybody. Neither rain nor snow nor dry bread would ever hurt them.

On Christmas Eve, Cobbler John returned late from his many errands. He had delivered all sorts of finished work and had collected a little money which he had to use to buy supplies and to pay for their daily needs. Hurrying homeward, he saw stands on every street corner, loaded with gold and silver lambs and candy dolls which pushcart women were selling as gifts for well-behaved children. Cobbler John stopped before one or two of the carts. . . . Maybe he ought to buy something. . . . What? For all nine? That would cost too much. Then for just one? And make the others envious? No, he'd give them another kind of Christmas present: a beautiful and good one, one that would neither break nor wear out, and which all could enjoy together and not take away from each other.

"Well, children! One, two, three, four . . . are you all here?" he said when he arrived home within the circle of his family of nine. "Do you know that this is Christmas Eve? A holiday, a very gay holiday. Tonight we do no work, we just rejoice!"

The children were so happy to hear that they were supposed to rejoice that they almost tore down the house.

"Wait now! Let's see if I can't teach you that beautiful song I know. It's a very beautiful song. I have saved it to give to you all as a Christmas present."

The little ones crawled noisily into their father's lap and up on his shoulders, and waited eagerly to hear the lovely song.

"Now what did I tell you? If you are good children—just stand nicely in line!—there, the bigger ones over here and the smaller ones next to them." He stood them in a row like organ pipes, letting the two smallest ones stay on his lap.

"And now—silence! First I'll sing it through, then you join in." Taking off his green cap and assuming a serious, pious expression, Cobbler John began to sing the beautiful melody: "On the blessed birth of our Lord Jesus Christ . . ."

The bigger boys and girls learned it after one rendition, though the smaller ones found it a bit more difficult. They were always off key and out of rhythm. But after a while they all knew it. And there could be no more joyous sound than when all the nine thin little voices sang together that glorious song of the angels on that memorable night. Perhaps the angels were still singing it when the melodious voices of nine innocent souls prayed for an echo from above. For surely there is gladness in heaven over the song of children.

But there was less gladness immediately above them. There, a bachelor was living all by himself in nine rooms. In one he sat, in the other one he slept, in the third one he smoked his pipe, in the fourth he dined, and who knows what he did in all the others? This man had neither wife nor children, but more money than he could count. Sitting in room number eight that night, this rich man was wondering why life had lost its taste. Why did his soft spring bed give him no peaceful dreams? Then, from Cobbler John's room below, at first faintly but with ever-increasing strength, came the strains of a certain joy-inspiring song. At first he tried not to listen, thinking they would soon stop. But

when they started all over for the tenth time, he could stand it no longer. Crushing out his expensive cigar, he went down in his dressing gown to the shoemaker's flat.

They had just come to the end of the verse when he walked in. Cobbler John respectfully got up from his three-legged stool and greeted the great gentleman.

"You are John, the cobbler, aren't you?" the rich man asked.

"That I am, and at your service, Your Excellency. Do you wish to order a pair of patent-leather boots?"

"That isn't why I came. How very many children you have!"

"Indeed, I have, Your Excellency—little ones and big ones. Quite a few mouths to feed!"

"And many more mouths when they sing! Look here, Master John—I'd like to do you a favor. Give me one of your children. I'll adopt him, educate him as my own son, take him traveling abroad with me, and make him into a gentleman. One day he'll be able to help the rest of you."

Cobbler John stared wide-eyed when he heard this. These were big words—to have one of his children made into a gentleman! Who wouldn't be taken by such an idea? Why, of course, he'd let him have one! What great good fortune! How could he refuse?

"Well, then, pick out one of them quickly, and let's get it over with," said the gentleman. Cobbler John started to choose.

"This one here is Alex. No, him I couldn't let go. He is a good student

and I want him to become a priest. The next one? That's a girl, and of course Your Excellency doesn't want a girl. Little Ference? He already helps me with my work. I couldn't do without him. Johnny? There, there—he is named after me. I couldn't very well give him away! Joseph? He is the image of his mother—it's as if I saw her every time I look at him. This place wouldn't be the same without him. And the next is another girl—she wouldn't do. Then comes little Paul: he was his mother's favorite. Oh, my poor darling would turn in her grave if I gave him away. And the last two are too small—they'd be too much trouble for Your Excellency. . . ."

He had reached the end of the line without being able to choose. Now he started all over, this time beginning with the youngest and ending with the oldest. But the result was still the same: he couldn't decide which one to give away because one was as dear to him as the other and he would miss them all.

"Come, my little ones—you do the choosing," he finally said. "Which one of you wants to go away to become a gentleman and travel in style? Come now, speak up! Who wants to go?"

The poor shoemaker was on the verge of tears as he asked them. But while he was encouraging them, the children slowly slipped behind their father's back, each taking hold of him, his hand, his leg, his coat, his leather apron, all hanging on to him, and hiding from the great gentleman. Finally Cobbler John couldn't control himself any longer. He knelt down, gathered them all into his arms and let his tears fall on their heads as they cried with him.

"It can't be done, Your Excellency! It can't be done. Ask of me anything in the world, but I can't give you a single one of my children so long as the Lord God has given them to me."

The rich gentleman said that he understood, but that the shoemaker should do at least one thing for him: Would he and his children please not sing any more? And for this sacrifice he asked Cobbler John to accept one thousand florins.

Master John had never even heard the words "one thousand florins" spoken, never in all his life. Now he felt the money being pressed into his hand.

His Excellency went back to his room and his boredom. And Cobbler John stood staring incredulously at the oddly shaped bank note. Then he fearfully locked it away in the wooden chest, put the key into his pocket, and was silent. The little ones were silent too. Singing was forbidden. The older children slumped moodily in their chairs, quieting the smaller ones by telling them they weren't allowed to sing any more because it disturbed the fine gentleman upstairs. Cobbler John himself was silently walking up and down. Impatiently he pushed aside little Paul, the one who had been his wife's favorite, when the boy asked that he be taught again that beautiful song because he had already forgotten how it went.

"We aren't allowed to sing any more!"

Then he sat down angrily at his bench and bent intently over his work. He cut and hammered and sewed until suddenly he caught himself humming: "On the blessed birth of our Lord Jesus Christ. . . ." He clapped his hand over his mouth. But then all at once he was very angry. He banged the hammer down on the workbench, kicked his stool from under him, opened the chest, took out the thousand-florin bill, and ran up the stairs to His Excellency's apartment.

"Good, kind Excellency, I am your most humble servant. Please take back your money! Let it not be mine, but let us sing whenever we please, because to me and my children that is worth much more than a thousand florins."

With that he put the bill down on the table and rushed breathlessly back to his waiting family. He kissed them one after the other; and lining them up in a row just like organ pipes, he sat himself down on his low stool, and together they began to sing again with heart and soul: "On the blessed birth of our Lord Jesus Christ. . . ." They couldn't have been happier if they had owned the whole of the great big house.

But the one who owned the house was pacing through his nine rooms, asking himself how it was that those people down below could be so happy and full of joy in such a tiresome, boring world as this!

GREECE

A frigid morning in mid-January: the wintry sun glints on the cold waves of the Hudson as a group of worshippers, shadowed by the skyscrapers of Manhattan, gather for the blessing of the waters. It is Epiphany, and around the world men and women of Greek descent have come together in much the same way to take part in a ceremony that is older than the celebration of Christ's birth. Though this ritual commemorating Christ's baptism brings Christmas to a close, in its quiet reverence it symbolizes the holiday as it is observed by Greeks the world over.

Indeed, it is Easter, and not Christmas, that stands as the great feast day in Greece; nevertheless, the Greek Christmas has a kind of austere beauty. As in many Old World countries, the holiday opens with the feast of St. Nicholas on December 6th, but there the similarities end. For the Greek St. Nicholas, patron saint of seamen, emerges as from a storm, his clothes and beard dripping with brine, his face covered with perspiration from the work of rescuing foundering ships. The industrious saint has no time to trifle with the delivery of presents, a job reserved for another holy man from Asia Minor, St. Basil, whose feast day falls later in the season, on January 1st.

Before St. Basil's Day, however, comes Christmas itself, ushered in to the sound of the *kalanda,* traditional Greek carols both religious and secular, sung by groups of boys who travel from house to house on Christmas Eve, accompanied by triangles and toy drums. Then comes the Christmas Eve meal, the focus of which is the *christpomo,* or Christ-bread, usually home-baked and lavishly decorated to reflect some special aspect of the family. The loaf is laid at the center of the table, along with a pot of honey and a cornucopia of dried fruits and nuts. After blessing it with the sign of the cross, the assembled guests lift up the table three times, in remembrance of the Trinity or the Holy Family. Particularly in rural areas, the Christmas Eve meal is associated with fertility and generosity. In Simitli, a small village in Thrace, nine different dishes are served on Christmas Eve; after blessing them with incense the family places them before a statue of Mary so that she may share in their bounty. Greek farm families place the Christmas table near the hearth, an ancient symbol of fertility, and cover the *christpomo* with a plate containing dried and fresh fruits, as well as wheat, garlic, coins, and a glass of ceremonial wine, thus ensuring a prosperous new year. The feasting continues on Christmas Day, again with *christpomo* and a traditional main dish of roast pork. Though the Christmas tree may be part of many Greek-American celebrations, it is noticeably absent in Greek tradition.

But Christmas Day in Greece is mere preface to the real feast days of St. Basil's Day and Epiphany. One of the four fathers of the Orthodox Church, Basil is also the patron saint of the poor and the homeless; perhaps because of his generosity, the day has become identified with the exchanging of Christmas gifts. Legend has it that Basil provided poor girls with dowries by baking a coin into a cake, which he then tossed through an open window. Today, these same cakes, the *vasilopita,* are baked on St Basil's Eve (in America, where the Greek and American traditions intermingle, the *vasilopita* appear on Christmas Eve as well); though the hidden coin hardly represents a dowry, the person fortunate enough to bite into it is assured a year of good luck.

The *vasilopita* coin is only one of a number of superstitions surrounding the Greek Christmas. As in many countries, primitive fears of dark spirits abroad in a time of dwindling light make themselves felt—here, in the form of the *Kallikanatzaroi,* goblins who emerge from the depths of the earth when the waters are yet unhallowed.

Epiphany banishes the *Kallikanatzaroi* to the darkness from which they came. For the Greeks it is a celebration, not just of Christ's baptism but of his birth as well—as it was for all Christians before the introduction of Christmas in the fourth century. As the sun reaches its highest point in the sky the priest blesses a small cross and tosses it gently into the waves—a sacred ceremony that takes place in Greek communities from the isle of Crete to Tarpon Springs, Florida. For all Greeks, this final day of the Christmas season represents not an ending but a renewal—of light and hope and the earth itself, as it turns toward spring.

CLAUDIA'S MOTHER'S
SPANAKOTIROPITA
(GREEK SPINACH AND CHEESE PITA)

Traditionally, a variety of *vasilopita*, dedicated to St. Basil, is served on New Year's Eve. A lucky coin (covered with foil) is placed inside the pita; the person who finds it will have good luck throughout the year. This recipe omits the coin, but you can certainly add it.

1   *package filo*
½ *pound sweet whipped butter*
2   *pounds fresh spinach*
5   *eggs*

1 *pound feta cheese*
1 *pound fresh ricotta cheese*
1 *pound cottage cheese*

Cut stalks off spinach and chop it fairly small. Soak cut-up spinach in water with salt to remove dirt. Change water 3 or 4 times until spinach is thoroughly clean. Squeeze out excess water and place spinach in a large deep bowl. Add cheeses and mix gently. Beat eggs in another bowl and pour over spinach mixture. Take the filo out of refrigerator, and place filo sheets over dampened towels. Melt butter on low heat, making sure it does not burn. Brush butter on bottom of roasting pan and place 6 or 7 sheets of filo on pan, brushing each lightly with butter. The pan should be the size of the filo sheets. Divide spinach mixture evenly over sheets. Place filo sheets over spinach mixture, brushing tops lightly with butter. Sprinkle lightly with water before putting in a 325 to 350 degree oven. Bake until brown, about 1 hour.

KOULOURAKIA
(GREEK COOKIES)

11–12 cups flour
1 tablespoon baking powder
¾ cup whipped sweet butter
8 eggs, separated
1½ cups sugar

1½ teaspoons vanilla
½ cup milk, warmed
1 egg, beaten
sesame seeds (optional)

Sift 11 cups of flour with the baking powder and sugar in it into a ceramic or glass bowl; scoop out a well in it. Brown the butter and pour into the flour's well. Let it stand until cool enough to handle. Rub the flour and the butter between the palms of your hands until well blended. Make another well in the middle of the mixture. Beat the egg yolks and vanilla until thick and light; beat the egg whites in another bowl until stiff. Add the yolks, the whites, and warm milk to the flour and knead to make a soft dough. Add more flour if needed; the dough should not stick to your hands. Taking a little dough at a time, roll out to quarter-inch thickness. Form into round doughnut shape or straight braided shape. Place on a buttered baking sheet, allowing enough space between cookies for them to expand. Brush tops with beaten egg and add sesame seeds if desired. Bake in a preheated 350 degree oven for about 20 minutes.

MAKES 10–11 DOZEN COOKIES

KOURAMBEADES
(GREEK COOKIES)

1 tablespoon butter
1 cup slivered and blanched almonds
1 cup sweet butter
1 cup Crisco
½ cup sugar

a few drops of vanilla
4 cups all purpose flour
a few drops of rosewater (optional)
confectioner's sugar

Melt butter in a skillet and toast almonds until brown. Cream butter and shortening. Add sugar and vanilla until thoroughly blended. Add flour one cup at a time, mixing after each addition. Add rosewater and almonds. Batter should resemble a coarse meal, but should stick together. If it is too sticky add flour. If it is too dry add butter. Divide mixture into three parts. Form one part into rounds, the second part into squares, and the third part into ovals. Make an indentation in the center of each cookie with your finger. Bake in a 350° oven until golden in color, 25–30 minutes. Cool the cookies. Then, using a sieve, coat thoroughly with confectioner's sugar.

MAKES ABOUT 4 DOZEN COOKIES

FRANCE

"*Joyeux Noël!*" ring out the voices, and "*Bon appetit!*"—for Christmas and feasting are practically synonymous in France. Christmas is a season of oysters and champagne, of roast goose and *roi de la fête,* of rich *boudin* and richer *bûche de Noël.* It is also a sacred season, a time when the music of church bells mingles with the sound of voices singing out the traditional French *noëls.* And as it is in France, so it is in French communities in North America, from New Orleans to Quebec City.

Until the second half of the nineteenth century, Christmas was almost entirely a religious holiday in France. Nevertheless, as in other countries, it retained elements of earlier pagan celebrations. In the countryside, Christmas traditionally began on December 4th, St. Barbar's Day; grain was planted in small dishes, and if it sprouted and grew by Christmas it presaged a bountiful harvest the following year. The *cosse de Nau,* the French yule log, was also believed to possess supernatural powers; each year a handful of ashes was preserved to keep the household safe from harm.

By the late nineteenth century the French had begun to absorb some of the festive spirit of both the English and the German holidays. The Christmas tree, a German invention, entered France through neighboring Alsace-Lorraine, and by the 1880's the English were exporting great quantities of mistletoe across the Channel. Today the holiday officially begins on December 5th, St. Nicholas Eve, which, along with New Year's Day, is the customary time for gift giving. Children leave their shoes by the hearth or, in hearthless homes, by the radiator, to be filled by the beneficent *Père Noël,* or Father Christmas.

A few days before Christmas, in houses and apartments throughout the country, the crèche is assembled. Of Italian origin, the crèche has been an integral and beloved part of the French holiday for at least four hundred years—which may explain why Americans use the French word to refer to the Nativity scene. Set up in a corner of the living room, the crèche is customarily decorated with evergreens and illuminated by candles (often tricolored, to represent the Trinity). Perhaps more than the tree itself, it is the centerpiece of the French celebration.

But it is Christmas Eve which is truly the center of the French holiday. A time for churchgoing and feasting, Christmas Eve is observed first at Midnight Mass and, afterward, at the *réveillon* supper, which breaks the day's fast. The traditional menu varies from region to region, but often consists of baked ham, roast fowl, various salads, cake, fruit, candies, and, of course, wine. In southwest France, oysters and champagne ring in the day of Christ's birth. Roast goose is popular in Alsace, while in Brittany buckwheat crepes with sour cream are traditional. *Boudin,* a hearty blood sausage, is eaten in Provence; and in Paris, the *réveillon* is often an elegant late supper of oysters and pâté.

Not surprisingly, on Christmas Day the French recuperate from the *réveillon* with yet another feast, typically consisting of oysters, pâté, a roast bird (often turkey, introduced to France from America, via England), potatoes, a vegetable, salad, cheese, wine, and abundant crusty French bread. Whatever the menu, custom dictates that the meal end with a *bûche de Noël,* a cylinder of sponge cake filled with buttercream fashioned to resemble a yule log. Iced with dark chocolate and often dotted with meringue mushrooms, the *bûche* does indeed resemble a miniature yule log. Perhaps because of its charming appearance (or its rich sweetness), it has become a common sight on American holiday tables as well.

The French celebration doesn't end with Christmas Day, but continues on into New Year's and Epiphany, both days of feasting. Whereas Christmas is a day for family celebrations, New Year's is a time for friends, for exchanging gifts and for sharing the New Year's *réveillon.* On Epiphany the family gathers together again, to eat the *galette* or *roi de la fête,* a flat flaky pastry into which has been baked a bean or a tiny china doll or sabot. The lucky diner whose portion contains the prize is declared King (or Queen) of the day, an honor usually accorded to younger members of the family. And so, to the clinking of glasses and the ringing of church bells, the rich feast that is Christmas in France comes to a festive close.

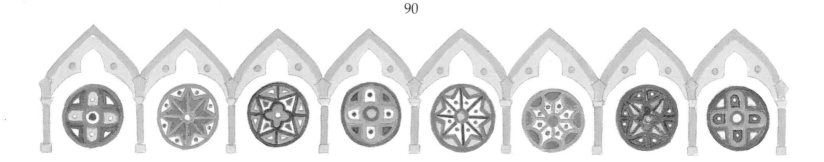

IL EST NÉ, LE DIVIN INFANT/ HE IS BORN, THE DIVINE CHILD
A Traditional French Carol

He is born, the Divine Child!
Play, oboes; sing, bagpipes!
He is born, the Divine Child!
Let us sing of His Advent!

For more than four thousand years,
The prophets promised Him to us;
For more than four thousand years,
We have awaited this joyous moment.

How fair He is, how charming,
How perfect are His features.
How fair He is, how charming,
How sweet, this Divine Child!
He is born, the Divine Child!
Play, oboes; sing, bagpipes!
He is born, the Divine Child!
Let us sing of His Advent!

CAROL OF THE BIRDS
Bas-Quercy

Whence comes this rush of wings afar,
Following straight the Noel star?
Birds from woods in wondrous flight
Bethlehem seek this Holy Night.

"Tell us, ye birds, why come ye here,
Into this stable, poor and drear?"
"Hast'ning we seek the newborn King,
And all our sweetest music bring."

Hark how the green-finch bears his
* part;*
Philomel, too, with tender heart,
Chants from her leafy dark retreat,
Re, mi, fa, sol, in accents sweet.

Angels and shepherds, birds of the sky,
Come where the Son of God doth lie;
Christ on the earth with man doth
* dwell,*
Join in the shout, Noel, Noel.

BÛCHE DE NOËL

This festive·dessert, which takes the form of a Yule log, is often served decorated with meringue mushrooms and a dusting of powdered sugar.

4 egg yolks, beaten
½ cup confectioner's sugar, sifted
1 teaspoon vanilla
4 tablespoons unsweetened cocoa
⅛ teaspoon salt

4 egg whites
1 cup heavy cream
2 tablespoons granulated sugar
½ teaspoon vanilla, or 2 tablespoons
   rum

Add the sugar to the egg yolks a little at a time and blend well. Add vanilla and cocoa. Whip together the salt and egg whites till they form stiff peaks and gently fold into batter. Pour into a large, lightly greased pan (about 9 × 12 inches), and bake in a preheated 325-degree oven for 25 to 30 minutes, or until a toothpick inserted in the center of the cake comes out dry. Set aside to cool.

Meanwhile, add the sugar and vanilla or rum to the cream and whip till spreadable. Cover the cake with whipped cream and gently roll into a log. Cover on all sides but bottom with icing (recipe below), swirling the knife to give the appearance of bark.

CHOCOLATE BUTTERCREAM ICING

2 ounces unsweetened chocolate
2 tablespoons butter
⅓ cup espresso, heated

2 cups confectioner's sugar, sifted
1 teaspoon cinnamon

In a double boiler melt the chocolate and butter. Remove double boiler top to a cool surface and add espresso. Slowly blend in sugar and cinnamon.

COLOMBES
(DOVE COOKIES)

1 cup flour
1 teaspoon baking powder
8 tablespoons butter, slightly softened

¼ cup sugar
1 egg yolk
1–2 tablespoons milk
currants

Preheat oven to 375 degrees. Combine sugar, butter, and egg, mixing lightly. Add baking powder to flour, mixing well. Add flour to butter and sugar mixture, and knead thoroughly, adding milk as necessary to make dough stiff. Chill, and roll out onto a floured board. Cut using a bird-shaped cookie cutter and place on an ungreased cookie sheet. Dot with currants for eyes. Bake for 10 minutes.

A CHRISTMAS IN THE FOREST
ANDRÉ THEURIET

Christmas Eve that year was bleak and cold, and the village seemed benumbed. The houses were closed hermetically, and so were the stables, from which came the muffled sound of animals chewing the cud. From time to time the clacking of wooden shoes on the hardened ground resounded through the deserted streets; then a door was hastily opened and closed, and all relapsed into silence. It was evident from the thick smoke rising through the chimneys into the gray air that every family was huddled around its hearth while the housewife prepared the Christmas supper. Stooping forward, with their legs stretched out to the fire, their countenances beaming with pleasure at the prospect of the morrow's festival and the fore-taste of the fat and juicy blood sausages, the peasants laughed at the north wind that swept the roads, at the frost that powdered the trees of the forest, and the ice that seemed to vitrify the streams and the river. Following their example, my friend Tristan and I spent the livelong day at the corner of the hearth in the old house of the Abbatiale, smoking our pipes 'and reading poetry. At sundown we had grown tired of seclusion and determined to venture out.

"The forest must be a strange sight with this heavy frost," said I to Tristan. "Suppose we take a turn through the wood after supper; besides, I must see the sabotiers from Courroy about a little matter."

So we pulled on our gaiters, stuffed our pipes, wrapped ourselves

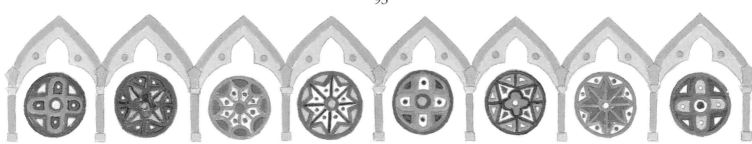

in our cloaks and mufflers, and penetrated into the wood.

We walked along cheerfully over the rugged, hardened soil of the trenches furrowed with deep, frozen ruts. Through the copse on either side, we saw mysterious white depths. After a damp night the north wind had transformed the mists and vapors that overhung the branches into a tangle of snowy lace. In the half night of the gloaming we could still distinguish the sparkling needles of the junipers, the frosted puffs of the clematis, the bluish crystallizations of the beech, and the silver filigree of the nut trees. The silence was broken by the occasional creaking of the frozen tree limbs, and every now and then a breath of impalpable white dust dampened our cheeks as it melted there.

We walked along at a steady pace, and in less than an hour caught sight of the red and flickering glow of the sabotiers' camp pitched on the edge of the forest above a stream that flowed down toward the valley of Santonge. The settlement consisted of a spacious, cone-shaped, dirt-coated hut and a cabin with board walls carefully sealed with moss. The hut answered the combined purposes of dormitory and kitchen; the cabin was used for the stowing away of tools and wooden shoes, and also for the two donkeys employed in the transportation of goods. The sabotiers, masters, apprentices, friends, and children were seated on beech logs around the fire

in front of the hut, and their mobile silhouettes formed intensely black profiles against the red of the fire. Three short posts driven into the ground and drawn together at the top formed the crane, from which hung an iron pot that simmered over the coals. An appetizing odor of stewed hare escaped from the tin lid as it rose and fell under the puffs of vapor. The master, a lively, nervous, hairy little man, welcomed us with his usual cordiality.

"Sit down and warm yourselves," said he. "You find us preparing the Christmas supper. I'm afraid we'll not sleep over-soundly tonight. My old woman is ill. I've fixed her a bed in the cabin where she'll be more comfortable, and warmer on account of the animals. My boy has gone to Santonge to get the doctor. There's no time to be lost. My little girl is kept busy running from the cabin to the hut."

We had no sooner taken our seats around the fire than the snowflakes began to whirl about in the stillness above us. They fell so thick and fast that in less than a quarter of an hour we were compelled to protect the fire with a hurdle covered with sack-cloth.

"By my faith! gentlemen," said the sabotier, "you'll not be able to start out again in this storm. You'll have to stay and have your Christmas supper with us——and taste of our stew."

The weather was certainly not tempting, and we accepted the

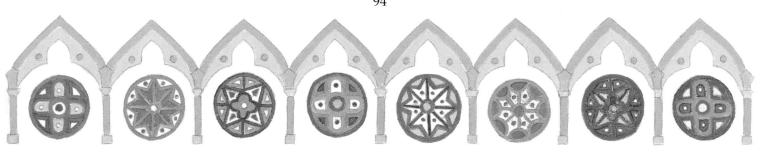

invitation. Besides, the adventure amused us, and we were delighted at the prospect of a Christmas supper, devouring our hare stew with a sharp appetite and washing it down with a draught of unfermented wine that scraped our throats. The snow fell thicker and thicker, wrapping the forest in a soft white wadding that deadened every sound. Now and then the sabotier rose and went into the cabin, then came back looking worried, listening anxiously for the good woman from Santonge. Suddenly a few metallic notes, muffled by the snow, rose softly from the depth of the valley. A similar sound from the opposite direction rang out in answer, then followed a third and a fourth, and soon a vague confusion of Christmas chimes floated over the forest.

Our hosts, without interrupting the process of mastication and while they passed around the wine jug, tried to recognize the various chimes by the fulness of the sounds.

"Those——now——those are the bells from Vivey. They are hardly any louder than the sound of the donkey's hoofs on the stones."

"That is the bell of Auberive!"

"Yes; and that peal that sounds like the droning of a swarm of beetles, that's the Grancey chimes."

During this discussion Tristan and I began to succumb to the combined action of warmth and fully satisfied appetite. Our eyes blinked, and before we knew it we fell asleep on the moss of the hut,

lulled by the music of the Christmas chimes. A piercing shriek followed by a sound of joyful voices woke us with a start.

It had ceased snowing. The night was growing pale, and through the little skylight we could see above the fleecy trees a faint light in the sky, where a belated star hung quivering.

"It is a boy!" shouted the master, bursting in upon us. "Gentlemen, if you think you would like to see him, why, I should be very glad; and it might bring him luck."

We went crunching over the snow after him to the cabin, lighted by a smoky lamp. On her bed of laths and moss lay the young mother, weak and exhausted, her head thrown back, her pale face framed by a mass of frowzy auburn hair. The "good woman," assisted by the little girl, was bundling up the newcomer, who wailed feebly. The two donkeys, amazed at so much stir and confusion, turned their kindly gray faces toward the bed, shook their long ears, and gazed around them with wide, intelligent eyes, blowing through their nostrils puffs of warm vapor that hung like a thin mist on the air. At the foot of the bed stood a young shepherd, with a black and white she-goat and a newborn kid.

"I have brought you the she-goat, Ma'am Fleuriot," said he, in his Langrois drawl. "You can have her for the boy as long as you wish."

The goat was baaing, the newborn child wailed, and the donkeys

breathed loudly. There was something primitive and biblical about the whole scene.

Without, in the violet light of the dawn, while a distant church bell scattered its early notes through the air, one of the young apprentices, dancing in the snow to keep warm, sang out at the top of his lungs that old Christmas carol, which seemed then full of new meaning and poetry:—

"He is born, the little Child.
   Ring out, hautbois! ring out,
      bagpipes!
He is born, the little Child.
   Let us sing the happy news."

THE MIRACLE OF THE FIR TREES
JEAN VARIOT

Once upon a time on a frosty Christmas Eve, in a small village, a little boy was wandering barefooted, from house to house.

"Would anyone like to buy two small fir trees? . . . You can decorate them with bright lights and paper stars . . . It's a lot of fun for the children," the boy would cry, as he knocked on a door.

At each house, the answer was always the same:

"You've come too late, child. We've already bought our Christmas tree. Come back again next year."

And each time, the boy would go away with tears in his eyes. If he didn't sell the two trees there would be nothing for his family to eat. His mother and father were both sick, and his two brothers were still babies. Albert was the only one in his family able to earn money. So, in spite of the bitter cold, he roved through the streets, looking for someone to buy his fir trees. He had found the trees on the edge of the woods, just as night began to fall, at the hour when hungry wolves began their howling.

After knocking on several doors, and receiving many blunt answers, the boy found himself at the house of Eidel, the gardener.

Can you imagine trying to sell fir trees to a man whose job it is to make them grow?

Albert knocked.

"Who is knocking at this hour?" Eidel's gruff voice replied.

By now, Albert was so afraid, he didn't dare say who he was or what he wanted.

"Who is it? Who is knocking at my door when I want to be left in peace?" grumbled Eidel, his wooden shoes clattering as he came along.

When the door opened, the boy saw a beautiful tree, glistening with gaily wrapped presents and decorations, whose bright glittering lit up the deserted street. At the other end of the room, there was a blazing fire in the hearth. And sitting near it, were three children looking from the hearth to the kitchen, where a juicy Christmas turkey lay on a table just waiting to be eaten.

96

"What do you want, little one?" Eidel asked the boy. "What are you doing with those two stunted fir trees?"

Albert didn't answer, as he thought he had just lost his last chance to earn money.

"The cold wind is blowing in," said the gardener. "Speak up, boy, or I'll have to close the door and leave you standing there."

Eidel had a rough way of speaking, but he was a good man. Looking at poor, frightened Albert standing in the snow, without any shoes, the gardener thought of his own children. They were about the same age as this boy. "If I were not here to look after them, some wintry night my children might be roaming the streets, too," he said to himself. But, kindly, he asked Albert, "What can I do for you?"

"I wanted to sell my fir trees for Christmas," said Albert, "but you already have such a beautiful one."

"Never mind!" Eidel answered. "All the same, I'll buy yours." And he went to get a gold coin from the drawer where he kept his savings.

"It's too good to be true," thought Albert. "The old gardener must be playing a joke on me, or maybe it's all a dream." But when each of the children gave him a slice of turkey and their mother brought out a piping hot bowl of soup, Albert knew he wasn't dreaming.

When he had finished eating, the boy thanked the kind gardener and his family. And, happy as a lark, he started home with Eidel's dog for

protection against the wolves.

On Christmas morning, after all the presents had been opened, Mrs. Eidel started cleaning up her house. She picked up all the wrappings, the ribbons, the decorations and put them away. Then she threw Albert's two fir trees into the street.

Her three children were playing in the street while waiting to go to church. When they saw their mother throw the fir trees out, they decided to pretend they were gardeners, just like their father. So they took the tres across the road and planted them behind the church.

Soon the church bells began to ring and crowds of people started pouring into the church. Eidel and his family were among the first to arrive. Dressed in his best clothes, Eidel sat with his wife and children in the front pew. The gardener reverently asked God to watch over his family. As the choir sang the glory and wonder of Our Lord's birth, it occurred to Eidel that the Infant born in a manager is the true brother of poor children. "One can never be too kind to them," the gardener thought.

Mass was over, the candles snuffed out and the last parishioners leaving, when, all at once, the crowd outside the church gasped in amazement. Reaching high above the steeple, as straight as masts of a ship, were two fir trees, towering to the sky. And all around their thick, heavy branches, doves, as white as snow, were singing the Glory of God.

RUSSIA

Deep forests of pine and silver birch, wooden cottages shuttered against the wind, a lone spire piercing the wintry sky, and everywhere snow, piling against the houses, blanketing the wheat fields, settling on the eaves for the long and relentless Russian winter. Little wonder, then, that the Russian Christmas has retained elements of pagan rituals celebrating sun and sky. Even in contemporary Russia, where so many of the old traditions have disappeared, echoes of these rituals remain. The Russian people have always embraced pageantry and celebration, and not even government policy can stamp out Christmas in the Russian soul. Here in America, in émigré communities from Chicago to New York's Brighton Beach, the old traditions have taken root and blossomed.

For centuries Nicholas of Myra was the patron saint of Russia,

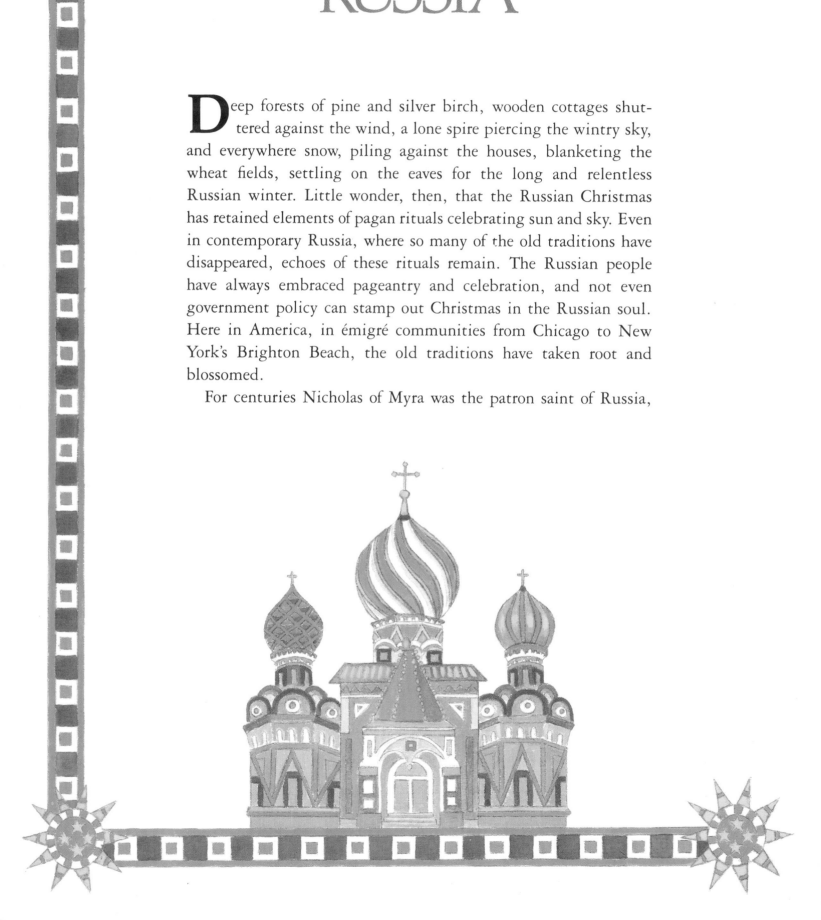

and as in other Eastern Orthodox countries, his feast day was observed with intense devotion. Today, however, the holiday season is more likely to begin with the first Sunday in Advent, a time of fasting for some (no meat is served for forty days before Christmas), but also a season of song and celebration. Especially popular, in Russia and among Americans of Russian descent, are the *Kolyádki*, ancient carols praising the sun, moon, and stars, or lauding the bountiful harvest. It was the sun goddess, Kolyáda, who gave her name not only to the songs of the season but to the Russian Christmas itself (also called *Kolyáda*). In some Russian-American households she still makes her Christmas Eve visit, dressed in white and gold like Germany's *Christkind,* to exchange gifts for carols. In old Russia, however, it was Babouschka who brought gifts to good children. Similar to the Italian Befana, Babouschka was visited by the Three Kings and was either too busy with her spinning to accompany them or deliberately misdirected them. In either case, gift-giving was the price she paid for her oversight, much to the gratification of Russian children. In Russia today, gifts are brought by Grandfather Frost, an old man who bears a striking resemblance to the European Father Christmas.

Christmas Eve signals the end of the Advent fast, as the family comes together for the *Colatzia,* or Christmas Eve supper. The meal begins with a thin wafer imprinted with scenes of the Nativity, still eaten in many Russian and Lithuanian families in America. The Russian appetite, traditionally hearty, indulges itself on Christmas Eve, with a meal that often includes pastrami, roast pork, and some sort of fowl, usually duck or goose. As in Poland, straw is scattered beneath the tablecloth to bring to mind Christ's birth in a manger. After dinner the family gathers round the Christmas tree, a symbol of joy and hope that not even the Revolution could entirely erase (though Russians in the U.S.S.R. know it now as the New Year's tree). In the days of the tsar, trees were decorated with apples and oranges, dolls made of candy and dried fruit, and foil-covered walnut meats dipped in egg white. Supper in old Russia would often be interrupted by the sound of carolers, usually boys, dressed as animals and carrying grains of wheat to toss across the threshold. They also carried a gilded star, perhaps representing an amalgam of Kolyáda and the star of Bethlehem.

Christmas Eve is the first of the *Svyatki,* or Holy Evenings, that continue through Epiphany. This is the traditional time of omens and divination, when the weather is believed to hold clues to the coming year's harvest (frost, for instance, presages plenty). It is also the season of the supernatural: Folk legend has it that the demons of the forest come out of hiding during the *Svyatki* to wreak havoc in the greater world. As in Greece, they are banished with the blessing of the waters, which takes place in Russian communities on Epiphany Eve. Across America, Russian Orthodox con-gregations come together at water's edge to watch the priest sanc-tify the water in a celebration of Christ's baptism. Though few Russian Americans give credence to the stories of marauding de-mons, the blessing—which closes the Russian Christmas—is both an important religious ritual and a cherished tie to the Russia of their forefathers.

RUSSIAN WAFERS

3 teaspoons baking powder
½ teaspoon salt
1 cup sweet butter
1 cup granulated sugar

2 eggs, beaten
2¼ teaspoons vanilla
2 cups flour, sifted

Mix together all ingredients but flour. Add flour little by little until well mixed and smooth. Chill for at least eight hours. Flour a pastry board and roll small bits of dough very thin until all dough has been rolled out. Cut in thin strips, topping each strip with a little granulated sugar. Bake in a preheated 400-degree oven until lightly browned. (These wafers were traditionally imprinted with Nativity scenes, but the stamps may be hard to come by. Imprinted or plain, they go very well with Russian tea, a recipe for which follows.)

RUSSIAN TEA

Traditionally, Russian tea is poured, steaming and strong, from a silver samovar. A pretty teapot will substitute rather nicely in the household missing a samovar.

1 pot of strongly brewed tea
lemon and orange slices
candied mint leaves

maraschino cherries, stuck with
    whole cloves
candied ginger

Arrange the sweets around the teapot on a large platter so that each guest can flavor his own cup of tea. Serve piping hot, with Russian wafers.

TRADITIONAL RUSSIAN KOLYADKA

Kolyada! Kolyada!
Kolyada has arrived.
On the eve of the Nativity,
Holy Kolyada.
Through all the courts, in all the
  alleys,
We found Kolyada
In Peter's Court.
Round Peter's Court there is an iron
  fence,
In the midst of the Court there are three
  rooms,
In the first room is the bright Moon,
In the second room the red Sun,
And in the third room, the many Stars.

WHERE LOVE IS, THERE GOD IS ALSO

LEO TOLSTOY

In the city lived the shoemaker, Martuin Avdyeitch. He lived in a basement, in a little room with one window. The window looked out on the street. Through the window he used to watch the people passing by; although only their feet could be seen, yet by the boots Martuin Avdyeitch recognized the people. Martuin Avdyeitch had lived long in one place, and had many acquaintances. Few pairs of boots in his district had not been in his hands once and again. Some he would half-sole, some he would patch, some he would stitch around, and occasionally he would also put on new uppers. And through the window he often recognized his work.

Avdyeitch had plenty to do, because he was a faithful workman, used good material, did not make exorbitant charges, and kept his word. If it was possible for him to finish an order by a certain time, he would accept it; otherwise, he would not deceive you—he would tell you so beforehand. And all knew Avdyeitch, and he was never out of work.

Avdyeitch had always been a good man; but as he grew old, he began to think more about his soul, and get nearer to God. Martuin's wife had died when he was still living with his master. His wife had left him a boy three years old. None of their other children had lived. All the eldest had died in childhood. Martuin at first intended to send his little son to his sister in the village, but afterward he felt sorry for him; he thought to himself:

"It will be hard for my Kapitoshka to live in a strange family. I shall keep him with me."

And Avdyeitch left his master, and went into lodgings with his little son. But God gave Avdyeitch no luck with his children. As Kapitoshka grew older, he began to help his father, and would have been a delight to him, but a sickness fell on him, he went to bed, suffered a week, and died. Martuin buried his son, and fell into despair. So deep was this despair that he began to complain of God. Martuin fell into such a melancholy state, that more than once he prayed to God for death, and reproached God because He had not taken him who was an old man, instead of his beloved only son. Avdyeitch also ceased to go to church.

And once a little old man from the same district came from Troïtsa to see Avdyeitch; for seven years he had been wandering about. Avdyeitch talked with him, and began to complain about his sorrows.

"I have no desire to live any longer," he said: "I only wish I was dead. That is all I pray God for. I am a man without anything to hope for now."

And the little old man said to him:

"You don't talk right, Martuin: we must not judge God's doings. The world moves, not by our skill, but by God's will. God decreed for your son to die—for you—to live. So it is for the best. And you are in despair, because you wish to live for your own happiness."

"But what shall one live for?" asked Martuin.

And the little old man said:

"We must live for God, Martuin. He gives you life, and for His sake you must live. When you begin to live for Him, you will not grieve over anything, and all will seem easy to you."

Martuin kept silent for a moment, and then said, "But how can one live for God?"

And the little old man said:

"Christ has tuaght us how to live for God. You know how to read? Buy a Testament, and read it; there you will learn how to live for God. Everything is explained there."

And these words kindled a fire in Avdyeitch's heart. And he went that very same day, bought a New Testament in large print, and began to read.

At first Avdyeitch intended to read only on holidays; but as he began to read, it so cheered his soul that he used to read every day. At times he would become so absorbed in reading, that all the kerosene in the lamp would burn out, and still he could not tear himself away. And so Avdyeitch used to read every evening.

And the more he read, the clearer he understood what God wanted of him, and how one should live for God; and his heart kept growing easier and easier. Formerly, when he lay down to sleep, he used to sigh and groan, and always thought of his Kapitoshka; and now his only exclamation was:

"Glory to Thee! Glory to Thee, Lord! Thy will be done."

And from that time Avdyeitch's whole life was changed. In other days he, too, used to drop into a public-house as a holiday amusement, to drink a cup of tea; and he was not averse to a little brandy either. He would take a drink with some acquaintance, and leave the saloon, not intoxicated exactly, yet in a happy frame of mind, and inclined to talk nonsense, and shout, and use abusive language at a person. Now he left off that sort of thing. His life became quiet and joyful. In the morning he would sit down to work, finish his allotted task, then take the little lamp from the hook, put it on the table, get his book from the

shelf, open it, and sit down to read. And the more he read, the more he understood, and the brighter and happier it grew in his heart.

Once it happened that Martuin read till late into the night. He was reading the Gospel of Luke. He was reading over the sixth chapter; and he was reading the verses:

"And unto him that smiteth thee on the one cheek offer also the other; and him that taketh away thy cloak forbid not to take thy coat also. Give to every man that asketh of thee; and of him that taketh away thy goods ask them not again. And as ye would that men should do to you, do ye also to them likewise."

He read farther also those verses, where God speaks:

"And why call ye me, Lord, Lord, and do not the things which I say? Whosoever cometh to me, and heareth my sayings, and doeth them, I will shew you to whom he is like: he is like a man which built an house, and digged deep, and laid the foundation on a rock: and when the flood arose, the stream beat vehemently upon that house, and could not shake it; for it was founded upon a rock. But he that heareth, and doeth not, is like a man that without a foundation built an house upon the earth; against which the stream did beat vehemently, and immediately it fell; and the ruin of that house was great."

Avdyeitch read these words, and joy filled his soul. He took off his spectacles, put them down on the book, leaned his elbows on the table, and became lost in thought. And he began to measure his life by these words. And he thought to himself:

"Is my house built on the rock, or on the sand? 'Tis well if on the rock. It is so easy when you are alone by yourself; it seems as if you had done everything as God commands; but when you forget yourself, you sin again. Yet I shall still struggle on. It is very good. Help me, Lord!"

Thus ran his thoughts; he wanted to go to bed, but he felt loath to tear himself away from the book. And he began to read farther in the seventh chapter. He read about the centurion, he read about the widow's son, he read about the answer given to John's disciples, and finally he came to that place where the rich Pharisee desired the Lord to sit at meat with him; and he read how the woman that was a sinner anointed His feet, and washed them with her tears, and how He forgave her. He reached the forty-fourth verse, and began to read:

"And he turned to the woman, and said unto Simon, Seest thou this woman? I entered into thine house, thou gavest me no water for my feet: but she hath washed my feet with tears, and wiped them with the hairs of her head. Thou gavest me no kiss: but this woman since the time I came in hath not ceased to kiss my feet. My head with oil thou didst not anoint:

but this woman hath anointed my feet with ointment."

He finished reading these verses, and thought to himself:

"Thou gavest me no water for my feet, thou gavest me no kiss. My head with oil thou didst not anoint."

And again Avdyeitch took off his spectacles, put them down on the book, and again he became lost in thought.

"It seems that Pharisee must have been such a man as I am. I, too, apparently have thought only of myself—how I might have my tea, be warm and comfortable, but never to think about my guest. He thought about himself, but there was not the least care taken of the guest. And who was his guest? The Lord Himself. If He had come to me, should I have done the same way?"

Avdyeitch rested his head upon both his arms, and did not notice that he fell asleep.

"Martuin!" suddenly seemed to sound in his ears.

Martuin started from his sleep:

"Who is here?"

He turned around, glanced toward the door—no one.

Again he fell into a doze. Suddenly he plainly heard:

"Martuin! Ah, Martuin! look tomorrow on the street. I am coming."

Martuin awoke, rose from the chair, began to rub his eyes. He himself could not tell whether he had heard those words in his dream, or in reality. He turned down his lamp, and went to bed.

At daybreak next morning, Avdyeitch rose, made his prayer to God, lighted the stove, put on the *shchi* and the kasha, put the water in the samovar, put on his apron, and sat down by the window to work.

And while he was working, he kept thinking about all that had happened the day before. It seemed to him at one moment that it was a dream, and now he had really heard a voice.

"Well," he said to himself, "such things have been."

Martuin was sitting by the window, and looking out more than he was working. When any one passed by in boots which he did not know, he would bend down, look out of the window, in order to see, not only the feet, but also the face.

The *dvornik* passed by in new felt boots, the watercarrier passed by; then there came up to the window an old soldier of Nicholas's time, in an old pair of laced felt boots, with a shovel in his hands. Avdyeitch recognized him by his felt boots. The old man's name was Stepanuitch; and a neighboring merchant, out of charity, gave him a home with him. He was required to assist the *dvornik*. Stepanuitch began to shovel away the snow from in front of Avdyeitch's window. Avdyeitch glanced

at him, and took up his work again.

"Pshaw! I must be getting crazy in my old age," said Avdyeitch, and laughed at himself. "Stepanuitch is clearing away the snow, and I imagine that Christ is coming to see me. I was entirely out of my mind, old dotard that I am!"

Avdyeitch sewed about a dozen stitches, and then felt impelled to look through the window again. He looked out again through the window, and saw that Stepanuitch had leaned his shovel against the wall, and was warming himself, and resting. He was an old broken-down man; evidently he had not strength enough even to shovel the snow. Avdyeitch said to himself:

"I will give him some tea; by the way, the samovar has only just gone out." Avdyeitch laid down an awl, rose from his seat, put the samovar on the table, poured out the tea, and tapped with his finger at the glass. Stepanuitch turned around, and came to the window. Avdyeitch beckoned to him, and went to open the door.

"Come in, warm yourself a little," he said. "You must be cold."

"May Christ reward you for this! My bones ache," said Stepanuitch.

Stepanuitch came in, and shook off the snow, tried to wipe his feet, so as not to soil the floor, but staggered.

"Don't trouble to wipe your feet. I will clean it up myself; we are used to such things. Come in and sit down," said Avdyeitch. "Here, drink a cup of tea."

And Avdyeitch filled two glasses, and handed one to his guest; while he himself poured his tea into a saucer, and began to blow it.

Stepanuitch finished drinking his glass of tea, turned the glass upside down, put the half-eaten lump of sugar on it, and began to express his thanks. But it was evident he wanted some more.

"Have some more," said Avdyeitch, filling both his own glass and his guest's. Avdyeitch drank his tea, but from time to time glanced out into the street.

"Are you expecting any one?" asked his guest.

"Am I expecting any one? I am ashamed even to tell whom I expect. I am, and I am not, expecting some one; but one word has kindled a fire in my heart. Whether it is a dream, or something else, I do not know. Don't you see, brother, I was reading yesterday the Gospel about Christ the Batyushka; how He suffered, how He walked on the earth. I suppose you have heard about it?"

"Indeed I have," replied Stepanuitch; "but we are people in darkness, we can't read."

"Well, now, I was reading about that very thing—how He walked on the earth; I read, you know, how He came to the Pharisee, and the Pharisee did not treat Him hospitably. Well, and so, my brother, I was reading yesterday, about this very thing, and was thinking to myself how he did not receive Christ the Batyushka, with honor. Suppose, for example, He should come to me, or any one else, I said to myself, I should not even know how to receive Him. And he gave Him no reception at all. Well! while I was thus thinking, I fell asleep, brother, and I heard some one call me by name. I got up; the voice, just as if some one whispered, said, 'Be on the watch; I shall come to-morrow.' And this happened twice. Well! would you believe it, it got into my head? I scolded myself—and yet I am expecting Him, the Batyushka."

Stepanuitch shook his head, and said nothing; he finished drinking his glass of tea, and put it on the side; but Avdyeitch picked up the glass again, and filled it once more.

"Drink some more for your good health. You see, I have an idea that, when the Batyushka went about on this earth, He disdained no one, and had more to do with the simple people. He always went to see the simple people. He picked out His disciples more from among folk like such sinners as we are, from the working class. Said He, whoever exalts himself, shall be humbled, and he who is humbled shall become exalted. Said He, you call me Lord, and, said He, I wash your feet. Whoever wishes, said He, to be the first, the same shall be a servant to all. Because, said He, blessed are the poor, the humble, the kind, the generous."

And Stepanuitch forgot about his tea; he was an old man, and easily moved to tears. He was listening, and the tears rolled down his face.

"Come, now, have some more tea," said Avdyeitch; but Stepanuitch made the sign of the cross, thanked him, turned down his glass, and arose.

"Thanks to you," he says, "Martuin Avdyeitch, for treating me kindly, and satisfying me, soul and body."

"You are welcome; come in again; always glad to see a friend," said Avdyeitch.

Stepanuitch departed; and Martuin poured out the rest of the tea, drank it up, put away the dishes, and sat down again by the window to work, to stitch on a patch. He kept stitching away, and at the same time looking through the window. He was expecting Christ, and was all the while thinking of Him and His deeds, and his head was filled with the different speeches of Christ.

Two soldiers passed by: one wore boots furnished by the crown, and the other one, boots that he had made; then the master of the next

house passed by in shining galoshes; then a baker with a basket passed by. All passed by; and now there came also by the window a woman in woolen stockings and rustic *bashmaks* on her feet. She passed by the window, and stood still near the window-case.

Avdyeitch looked up at her from the window, and saw it was a stranger, a woman poorly clad, and with a child; she was standing by the wall with her back to the wind, trying to wrap up the child, and she had nothing to wrap it up in. The woman was dressed in shabby summer clothes; and from behind the frame, Avdyeitch could hear the child crying, and the woman trying to pacify it; but she was not able to pacify it.

Avdyeitch got up, went to the door, ascended the steps, and cried:

"My good woman. Hey! my good woman!"

The woman heard him and turned around.

"Why are you standing in the cold with the child? Come into my room, where it is warm; you can manage it better. Here, this way!"

The woman was astonished. She saw an old, old man, in an apron, with spectacles on his nose, calling her to him. She followed him. They descended the steps and entered the room; the old man led the woman to his bed.

"There," said he, "sit down, my good woman, nearer to the stove; you can get warm, and nurse the little one."

"I have no milk for him. I myself have not eaten anything since morning," said the woman; but, nevertheless, she took the baby to her breast.

Avdyeitch shook his head, went to the table, brought out the bread and a dish, opened the oven-door, poured into the dish some cabbage-soup, took out the pot with the gruel, but it was not cooked as yet; so he filled the dish with *shchi* only, and put it on the table. He got the bread, took the towel down from the hook, and spread it upon the table.

"Sit down," he said, "and eat, my good woman; and I will mind the little one. You see, I once had children of my own; I know how to handle them."

The woman crossed herself, sat down at the table, and began to eat; while Avdyeitch took a seat on the bed near the infant. Avdyeitch kept smacking and smacking to it with his lips; but it was a poor kind of smacking, for he had no teeth. The little one kept on crying. And it occurred to Avdyeitch to threaten the little one with his finger; he waved, waved his finger right before the child's mouth, and hastily withdrew it. He did not put it to its mouth, because his finger was black, and soiled with wax. And the little one looked at his finger, and became quiet; then it began to smile, and Avdyeitch also was glad. While the woman was eating, she told who she was, and whither she was going.

Said she:

"I am a soldier's wife. It is now seven months since they sent my husband away off, and no tidings. I lived out as cook; the baby was born; no one cared to keep me with a child. This is the third month that I have been struggling along without a place. I ate up all I had. I wanted to engage as a wet-nurse—no one would take me—I am too thin, they say. I have just been to the merchant's wife, where lives a young woman I know, and so they promised to take us in. I thought that was the end of it. But she told me to come next week. And she lives a long way off. I got tired out; and it tired him too, my heart's darling. Fortunately our landlady takes pity on us for the sake of Christ, and gives us a room, else I don't know how I should manage to get along."

Avdyeitch sighed, and said:

"Haven't you any warm clothes?"

"Now is the time, friend, to wear warm clothes; but yesterday I pawned my last shawl for a twenty-kopek piece."

The woman came to the bed, and took the child: and Avdyeitch rose, went to the partition, rummaged round, and succeeded in finding an old coat.

"Na!" says he; "it is a poor thing, yet you may turn it to some use."

The woman looked at the coat and looked at the old man; she took the coat, and burst into tears; and Avdyeitch turned away his head; crawling under the bed, he pushed out a little trunk, rummaged in it, and sat down again opposite the woman.

And the woman said:

"May Christ bless you, little grandfather! He must have sent me to your window. My little baby would have frozen to death. When I started out it was warm, but now it has grown cold. And He, the Batyushka, led you to look through the window and take pity on me, an unfortunate."

Avdyeitch smiled, and said:

"Indeed, He did that! I have been looking through the window, my good woman, for some wise reason."

And Martuin told the soldier's wife his dream, and how he heard the voice—how the Lord promised to come and see him that day.

"All things are possible," said the woman. She rose, put on the coat, wrapped up her little child in it; and, as she started to take leave, she thanked Avdyeitch again.

"Take this, for Christ's sake," said Avdyeitch, giving her a twenty-kopek piece; "redeem your shawl."

She made the sign of the cross, and Avdyeitch made the sign of the cross and went with her to the door.

The woman went away. Avdyeitch ate some *shchi,* washed the dishes, and sat down again to work. While he was working he still remembered the window; when the window grew darker he immediately looked out to see who was passing by. Acquaintances passed by and strangers passed by, and there was nothing out of the ordinary.

But here Avdyeitch saw that an old apple-woman had stopped in front of his window. She carried a basket with apples. Only a few were left, as she had evidently sold them nearly all out; and over her shoulder she had a bag full of chips. She must have gathered them up in some new building, and was on her way home. One could see that the bag was heavy on her shoulder; she tried to shift it to the other shoulder. So she lowered the bag on the sidewalk, stood the basket with the apples on a little post, and began to shake down the splinters in the bag. And while she was shaking her bag, a little boy in a torn cap came along, picked up an apple from the basket, and was about to make his escape; but the old woman noticed it, turned around, and caught the youngster by his sleeve. The little boy began to struggle, tried to tear himself away; but the old woman grasped him with both hands, knocked off his cap, and caught him by the hair.

The little boy was screaming, the old woman was scolding. Avdyeitch lost no time in putting away his awl; he threw it upon the floor, sprang to the door—he even stumbled on the stairs, and dropped his spectacles—and rushed out into the street.

The old woman was pulling the youngster by his hair, and was scolding, and threatening to take him to the policeman; the youngster was defending himself, and denying the charge.

"I did not take it," he said; "what are you licking me for? Let me go!"

Avdyeitch tried to separate them. He took the boy by his arm, and said:

"Let him go, babushka; forgive him, for Christ's sake."

"I will forgive him so that he won't forget it till the new broom grows. I am going to take the little villain to the police."

Avdyeitch began to entreat the old woman:

"Let him go, babushka," he said, "he will never do it again. Let him go, for Christ's sake."

The old woman let him loose; the boy started to run, but Avdyeitch kept him back.

"Ask the babushka's forgiveness," he said, "and don't you ever do it again; I saw you take the apple."

The boy burst into tears, and be-

gan to ask forgiveness.

"There now! that's right; and here's an apple for you."

And Avdyeitch took an apple from the basket, and gave it to the boy.

"I will pay you for it, babushka," he said to the old woman.

"You ruin them that way, the good-for-nothings," said the old woman. "He ought to be treated so that he would remember it for a whole week."

"Eh, babushka, babushka," said Avdyeitch, "that is right according to our judgment, but not according to God's. If he is to be whipped for an apple, then what ought to be done to us for our sins?"

The old woman was silent.

And Avdyeitch told her the parable of the master who forgave a debtor all that he owed him, and how the debtor went and began to choke one who owed him.

The old woman listened, and the boy stood listening.

"God has commanded us to forgive," said Avdyeitch, "else we, too, may not be forgiven. All should be forgiven, and the thoughtless especially."

The old woman shook her head, and sighed.

"That's so," said she; "but the trouble is that they are very much spoiled."

"Then, we who are older must teach them," said Avdyeitch.

"That's just what I say," remarked the old woman. "I myself have had seven of them—only one daughter is left."

And the old woman began to relate where and how she lived with her daughter, and how many grandchildren she had. "Here," she says, "my strength is only so-so, and yet I have to work. I pity the youngsters—my grandchildren—but what nice children they are! No one gives me such a welcome as they do. Aksintka won't go to any one but me. 'Babushka, dear babushka, loveliest.' "

And the old woman grew quite sentimental.

"Of course, it is a childish trick. God be with him," said she, pointing to the boy.

The woman was just about to lift the bag up on her shoulder, when the boy ran up, and said:

"Let me carry it, babushka; it is on my way."

The old woman nodded her head, and put the bag on the boy's back.

And side by side they passed along the street.

And the old woman even forgot to ask Avdyeitch to pay for the apple. Avdyeitch stood motionless, and kept gazing after them; and he heard them talking all the time as they walked away. After Avdyeitch saw them disappear, he returned to his room; he found his eye-glasses on the stairs—they were not broken; he picked up his awl, and sat down to work again.

After working a little while, it grew darker, so that he could not see to sew; he saw the lamplighter passing by to light the street-lamps.

"It must be time to make a light," he said to himself; so he got his little lamp ready, hung it up, and betook himself again to he work. He had one boot already finished; he turned it around, looked at it: "Well done." He put away his tools, swept off the cuttings, cleared off the bristles and ends, took the lamp, set it on the table, and took down the Gospels from the shelf. He intended to open the book at the very place where he had yesterday put a piece of leather as a mark, but it happened to open at another place; and the moment Avdyeitch opened the Testament, he recollected his last night's dream. And as soon as he remembered it, it seemed as if he heard some one stepping about behind him. Avdyeitch looked around, and saw—there, in the dark corner, it seemed as if people were standing; he was at a loss to know who they were. And a voice whispered in his ear:

"Martuin—ah, Martuin! did you not recognize me?"

"Who?" exclaimed Avdyeitch.

"Me," repeated the voice. "It was I;" and Stepanuitch stepped forth from the dark corner; he smiled, and like a little cloud faded away, and soon vanished. . . .

"And it was I," said the voice.

From the dark corner stepped forth the woman with her child; the woman smiled, the child laughed, and they also vanished.

"And it was I," continued the voice; both the old woman and the boy with the apple stepped forward; both smiled and vanished.

Avdyeitch's soul rejoiced; he crossed himself, put on his spectacles, and began to read the Evangelists where it happened to open. On the upper part of the page he read:

"For I was ahungered, and ye gave me meat: I was thirsty, and ye gave me drink: I was a stranger, and ye took me in.". . .

And on the lower part of the page he read this:

"Inasmuch as ye have done it unto one of the least of these my brethren, ye have done it unto me" (St. Matthew, chap. xxv).

And Avdyeitch understood that his dream had not deceived him; that the Savior really called on him that day, and that he really received Him.

MEXICO

Christmas in Mexico is a blaze of color—from the *piñatas* in their brilliant paper plumage to the scarlet-leaved poinsettias that crowd every outdoor market and florist's window. That same color spills across the border, into Mexican-American communities in California and throughout the Southwest. If Christmas in Arizona and New Mexico—and large parts of Texas, Colorado, and California—has a special flavor, that flavor is overwhelmingly Mexican. And every American can thank our neighbors to the south for at least one ubiquitous sign of the season: In 1829 Joel Robert Poinsett, U.S. ambassador to Mexico, returned home with a shipment of the russet-blossomed plants that today bear his name.

From the Spanish founding fathers, the Mexicans inherited a love of the dramatic that pervades the Mexican Christmas. With their history of public mystery and miracle plays—the medieval *autos sacramentales*—the Spanish padres arriving in Mexico naturally looked toward drama to convert the local Indians. What began as a theatrical lesson in Christianity grew into the most important expression of the Mexican Christmas—the ritual of the *posadas*. Beginning on December 16th and continuing through the next

eight evenings until Christmas Eve, Mexicans and Mexican-Americans reenact the Holy Family's search for shelter (*posadas* literally meaning "inns"). In each of the first eight *posadas* family members, representing innkeepers and pilgrims, play out the story of frustration on the road to Bethlehem. To Joseph's every inquiry comes the same answer: "No room at the inn." But then, miraculously on Christmas Eve, the final innkeeper recognizes the holy couple and joyfully offers them shelter. In some parts of the country the "pilgrims" travel from house to house, visiting friends and asking the traditional *posadas* question: "Who will give shelter to those travelers who come with their songs of walking the roads?" In either case, the ritual ends on Christmas Eve, with song, celebration, and—to the great delight of children from Mexico City to Santa Fe—the game of the *piñata*.

En las noches de posadas la piñata es lo mejor, goes the popular carol ("On the night of the *posadas,* the *piñata* is the best"), and few children would disagree. Traditionally of terra-cotta, and covered with fluttering strips of colored paper, *piñatas* come in a dazzling variety of incarnations, from birds and donkeys to human figures and jet planes. No matter what their shape, the object of the game is the same: Each child is blindfolded, provided with a stick, and set out to shatter the *piñata,* which has been suspended from the ceiling by a string. The point of this gleeful destruction is to set free the gifts and candies hidden in the *piñata*'s heart (*Dale, dale, dale!* the carol exhorts—"Hit it, hit it, hit it!"). Once again, it is the Spanish padres who must take credit for the *pinata*'s current role in the Christmas celebration. The tradition originated with the Aztecs, who placed offerings to their war god in small clay pots decorated with feathers. No doubt remembering the *pignata,* a gift-filled pouch popular at masked balls during the Italian Renaissance, the padres simply Christianized the Aztec custom.

Another exuberant expression of the Christmas spirit is the *farolitos*—paper lanterns that line sidewalks and windowsills and perch on the rooftops and walls of public buildings. The first *farolitos* made their way into Mexico on the ships of Spanish traders from the Philippines, whose business with the Chinese undoubtedly familiarized them with the ornate paper lanterns of the Orient. It was the American citizens of New Mexico, however, who gave the *farolitos* their current twist: Instead of expensive imported rice paper, the candles are set in brown paper bags, carefully cut to cast decorative shadows. Christmastime visitors to New Mexico are consistently charmed by the spectacle of the *farolitos*—so much so that the custom is increasingly embraced throughout the Southwest by Americans of every ethnic background.

In contrast with the pre-Christmas revelry, Christmas Day—as in many Catholic countries—is quiet, a time for churchgoing and family gatherings. The Christmas meal often begins with oxtail soup, enriched with beans and fired with chili; as in North America, the traditional main course is roast turkey, stuffed with bread and apples, and served with a colorful holiday salad of fresh fruit and vegetables. Other festive foods, enjoyed in Mexican homes on both sides of the border, include spareribs in a green chili sauce, the little meat pies known as *empañaditas,* a variety of enchiladas, and *marquesote*—an elegant cake made mainly from egg whites and whipping cream.

After Christmas the festive spirit makes itself felt once again, culminating at Epiphany. Though many Mexican children (and American children of Mexican descent) have already received their gifts from Santa Claus, still others wait for the Twelfth-Night visit of the Three Kings, leaving their shoes on the windowsill with great expectation. From the first of the *posadas* till late on Epiphany night, the Mexican Christmas, in light and pageantry, *se alborata con ardor*—"bursts forth with joy."

LAS POSADAS

Following is a traditional reading of the *posadas* ceremony, which begins with the song of the pilgrims:

Quien les da posada
a estos peregrinos,
que vienen cansados
de andar los caminos?

(Who will give shelter
to these travelers
who come singing
of walking the roads?)

1st INNKEEPER
Even though you say you're worn out,
we don't give shelter to those we don't
know.

JOSEPH
In the name of heaven, I ask for shelter,
since my beloved wife can no longer
walk.

INNKEEPER
Here there is no inn, so keep on
walking; I can't open up for just any
rogue.

CHORUS
Don't be inhumane; have a heart. God
will reward you.

INNKEEPER
Better leave now and stop bothering me,
because if you anger me, I'll beat you.

JOSEPH
Weary and worn we go on our way,
Lodging to seek whenever we may;

A carpenter from Nazareth I am,
Journeying afar to Bethlehem.
Mary, my loved one, needs shelter
tonight—
We beg you to help us, in our sad
plight.

CHORUS
He asks for shelter, beloved innkeeper, for
only one night, for the Queen of Heaven.

JOSEPH
My wife is Mary, the Queen of Heaven,
who soon will become mother of Christ,
the Holy Word.

INNKEEPER
Is it you, Joseph?
And your wife, Mary?
Come in, wanderers,
I didn't recognize you.
We'll give you shelter
with great joy;
come in, good Joseph,
come in with Mary.

Come in, holy wanderers;
receive this ovation,
there is nothing in this poor dwelling
but my heart.

CHORUS
This is a joyful night,
of pleasure and rejoicing
because here we give shelter
to the Mother of the Son of God.

TRADITIONAL MEXICAN CAROL

En las noches de posadas
la piñata es lo mejor;
la niña màs remilgada
se alborota con ardor.
Dale, dale, dale!
No pierdas el ti no quede la
distancia se pierde el camino.

On the night of posadas
the piñata *is the best;*
the shyest little girl
bursts forth with joy.
Hit it, hit it, hit it!
Don't lose the aim that
gives the distance.

MEXICAN CHRISTMAS COOKIES

1 cup butter, creamed	¾ teaspoon salt
1 cup granulated sugar	1½ teaspoons cinnamon
½ cup light brown sugar	½ teaspoon crushed cardamom seed
zest of one orange	½ cup ground walnuts
1 egg	⅓ cup orange juice
4 cups all-purpose flour, sifted	

Beat together the butter, sugar, zest, and egg. Add the rest of the ingredients, mixing thoroughly. Roll out very thin on a floured board and cut with Christmas cookie cut-ters. Bake in a preheated 425-degree oven for 7 minutes or so, until delicately browned.

MAKES ABOUT 120 cookies

MEXICAN CHRISTMAS SALAD

1 cup cooked sliced beets
1 large avocado, peeled and sliced
2 large oranges, peeled and sectioned
1 large banana, sliced
the fruit of 1 large pomegranate

1½ cups pineapple chunks
2 apples, cored and sliced, with peel
½ cup unsalted peanuts, chopped
1 head iceberg lettuce
vinaigrette dressing

Toss together the fruits and vegetables and top with vinaigrette. Serve cold.

SERVES 6 TO 8

MEXICAN OXTAIL SOUP

1 large oxtail
2 quarts water
2 cups cooked garbanzo beans
¼ cup olive oil

1 large onion, minced
Salt and freshly ground black pepper
chili sauce
1 tablespoon cilantro, finely minced

Place oxtail and water in a soup pot and bring to the boil; reduce heat and simmer, uncovered, for at least 1½ hours, preferably longer, until meat is very tender and broth is flavorful. Remove the oxtail and strip meat from the bone; return meat to the broth. Grind the garbanzo beans by hand or in a food processor and add to broth. Heat the oil in a skillet and saute the onion until golden; add to the broth. Season to taste with salt and pepper and bring to the boil once again. Serve with a swirl of chili sauce and a garnish of cilantro.

SERVES 10

AUSTRIA AND GERMANY

Nowhere is Christmas celebrated with more enthusiasm than in Germany and Austria. From the big cities with their bustling Christmas markets, to small Bavarian towns whose Christmas lights glitter against the snow, to the Austrian Alps where wooden houses are decked with ears of dried corn and garlands of spruce, Germany and neighboring Austria celebrate the holiday with characteristic spirit. Of their many contributions to an American Christmas, none is more significant than the Germans' unbounded zeal for the holiday.

It was that wholehearted embrace of Christmas and its festivities that brought into being what has become for Americans the most

122

enduring secular symbol of the season, the Christmas tree. For thousands of years—even before the birth of Christ—northern Europeans marked the winter solstice by filling the house with evergreens—laurel, holly, ivy, pine, and moss (which German children still incorporate into hearthside nativity scénes). The Germans combined this custom with the tradition of lighting Christmas candles to create the world's first Christmas trees. Though the tree's invention is often attributed to Martin Luther, it probably first appeared in the early seventeenth century, some fifty years or so after the great reformer's death. The custom traveled well: A century later it was firmly established in Finland, and not long after that, in Denmark and Norway. Prince Albert, of German descent, set up the first Christmas tree at Windsor Castle in 1841, and by century's end trees shimmered in sitting rooms from Moscow to Maine.

The earliest German trees were lit with candles and hung with apples, candies, small cakes, and cut-paper roses. Then, around 1880, Thuringian glassblowers developed a technique for creating glass balls and other figures of extraordinary delicacy, their interior shells coated with silver to give them an ethereal sheen. Another technique turned strands of glass into angels' hair and silver stars; all of these ornaments, of course, found their way onto German Christmas trees. The tree that presides over the American living room today is almost wholly German in appearance, from the tinsel strewn on its boughs (first made from aluminum foil in Northern

Germany in the nineteenth century) to the angel at its peak (a custom with roots in eighteenth-century Hamburg and Berlin). Among Moravian communities in Bethlehem, Pennsylvania, and Winston-Salem, North Carolina, another German tradition still thrives—*putzing*, the creation of tiny human and animal figures to hang on the tree.

But though the tree may dominate Christmas in the German heart, the holiday begins long before the tree's unveiling on Christmas Eve. Advent wreaths and candles appear in churches on the fourth Sunday before Christmas, and Advent calendars are hung in homes throughout the country in anticipation of the holiday. Advent, and its joyous anticipation of Christmas Day, has long been a part of the German celebration, as the words of this sixteenth-century Bavarian carol (anglicized by Barnaby Googe) attest:

Three weeks before the day whereon was born the Lord of Grace,
And on the Thursdaye, boys and girls do runne in every place,
And bounce and beat at every doore, with blows and lustie snaps,
And crie the Advent of the Lord, not born as yet, perhaps,
And wishing to the neighbours all, that in the houses dwell,
A happy yeare, and everything to spring and prosper well.

Advent is also the time of Germany's famous Christmas markets, whose stalls overflow with a wealth of holiday specialties, from trees and decorations to sausages and gingerbread. A celebrated letter by Germany's greatest poet, Johann Wolfgang von Goethe, was inspired by the Christmas market in Frankfurt; early one Christmas morning, by the light of a candle, he wrote to his friend Johann Christian Kestner: "As I went across the market and saw the many lights and toys, I thought of you. . . ." On a smaller scale, Christmas bazaars, often sponsored by church congregations, open their doors on December 1st; German churches in America have continued the custom, with bazaars beginning just after Thanksgiving.

As in other European countries, the holiday observances continue with St. Nicholas Day, December 6th, and for many Ger

and not Christmas Eve, is the time for gift-giving. In
.y St. Nicholas exchanged his bishop's robes for a fur-
.ned cloak in the sixteenth century when the Protestant Refor-
.ation tried to sweep away all traces of the papacy. As the patron
saint of children, however, Nicholas continued to distribute presents to good youngsters and switches (borne by his attendant, the
evil-looking Knecht Ruprecht) to the naughty. In many German
households, it isn't St. Nicholas who fills the children's shoes with
gifts but the *Christkind* (Christ child). Arriving in some areas of the
country on St. Nicholas Eve, in others on Christmas Eve, the
Christkind comes dressed in white robes, with a crown of gold to
match his golden wings. While the *Christkind* tradition hasn't
become ensconced in America, a common corruption of his name,
Kris Kringle, is familiar across the land as a synonym for Santa
Claus.

Weihnachtsabend (Christmas Eve) is the jewel of the German
holiday season, the day on which the family gathers together for
feasting and singing and—most important of all—admiring the
newly revealed Christmas tree. Secreted behind locked doors, the
parents decorate the tree and, in many families, spread below it the
presents brought by the Christ child. At six o'clock the doors are
flung open and all those assembled are duly dazzled by the spectacle
of tinsel and glory. Gifts are exchanged, Christmas poems are
recited, and, of course, carols are sung.

Music, appropriately, is the common thread that runs
throughout the German and Austrian Christmas, whether celebrated in Vienna or Munich, Alsace-Lorraine or the Tyrol. Much of
our most cherished Christmas music is of German origin, from
Bach's "Christmas Oratorio" and Handel's "Messiah" to Mohr and
Gruber's "Silent Night" and the traditional "O Tannenbaum!" The
lovely "Lo! How a Rose Ere Blooming," written in the fourteenth
century, is part of a large group of German songs celebrating the
Holy Mother and Child. In the sixteenth century Martin Luther
helped to expand the body of German Christmas music by adapting
traditional folk songs to suit the sacred message of the season. But
it was a church organist named Franz Xavier Gruber and an

assistant priest named Joseph Mohr who produced the German carol most often sung in American homes and churches. Composed in 1818, "Silent Night" had become a classic throughout Europe by mid-century; during World War I American soldiers stationed in Germany were sufficiently moved by the hymn to bring it back with them to America.

And if German tradition has filled our hearts with song, it has also filled our serving boards with food, particularly Christmas sweets. Gingerbread and marzipan are the most famous of these; indeed, every German bakery in the United States boasts a window full of marzipan, fashioned in the shape of fruits and animals, from Advent to Epiphany. *Pfeffernüsse* (pepper nuts) are now widely sold throughout America, even in suburban supermarkets—though the pepper that gives them their name is often replaced by ginger, cloves, and nutmeg. For at least six hundred years, *stollen,* a sweet bread made with liquor and candied fruits, has been baked at Christmastime; some say the wedge-shaped bread is meant to symbolize the Christ child wrapped in swaddling clothes. And the Germans are responsible for yet another enduring symbol of Christmas both beautiful and edible: the gingerbread house. With its gables covered in snowy icing and its walls studded with candies of every description, the gingerbread house stands as a symbol of the rich and glorious German Christmas.

How the Fir Tree Became the Christmas Tree

By Hedwig Liebkind

When the Christmas tree is lighted up, you are all happy, and may not stop to think how it comes, and that it is always a Fir tree which Father Christmas chooses. You think it quite natural, don't you? The Fir looks so proud and majestic in its glory! But the tree is really a modest one, and it is only through its humility that it became the chosen Christmas tree. And this is how it happened.

At the time when the Christ child was born all people, animals, trees and other plants were very happy. The Child was born to bring peace and goodwill to all beings. Daily people came to see the little one and always brought presents with them. Three trees, which stood near the crypt, saw the many people and thought they would like to give presents to the Child also.

The Palm said: "I will choose my biggest leaf and place it as a fan over the Child."

"And I," said the Olive, "I will sprinkle sweet smelling oil above him."

"What can I give to the Child?" asked the Fir.

"You?" the others said, "you have nothing to offer. Your needles would prick the wee baby and your tears are sticky."

This made the poor Fir very unhappy, indeed, and it said: "Yes, you are right. I have really nothing that would be good enough for the Christ child."

Now, quite near the trees had stood an Angel, who had heard all that the trees had said, and he was sorry for the Fir, who was so lowly and without envy of the other trees. He made up his mind at once to help the Fir, so when it grew dark and the stars came out, he begged a few of the little ones to come down and rest upon its branches. They did as the Angel asked them, and the light shone beautifully from the tree. At this very moment the Christ child opened his eyes, and as the lovely light fell upon him he smiled.

As he grew bigger and saw that the people celebrated his birthday every year by giving presents to each other, he asked Father Christmas to place a Fir tree in every house as well. Decorated with candles, it should shine for the children just as the stars had shone for him on his first birthday. Father Christmas did as he was asked, you may be sure.

So the Fir tree was rewarded for its meekness, for surely there is no other tree that shines on so many happy faces.

THE GOLDEN COBWEBS
A Tale for Small Children

I am going to tell you a story about something wonderful that happened to a Christmas tree like this, ever and ever so long ago, when it was once upon a time.

It was before Christmas, and the tree was all trimmed with popcorn and silver nuts and [name the trimmings of the tree before you], and stood safely out of sight in a room where the doors were locked, so that the children should not see it before it was time. But ever so many other little house-people had seen it. The big black pussy saw it with her great green eyes; the little gray kitty saw it with her little blue eyes; the kind house-dog saw it with his steady brown eyes; the yellow canary saw it with his wise, bright eyes. Even the wee, wee mice that were so afraid of the cat had peeped one peek when no one was by.

But there was someone who hadn't seen the Christmas tree. It was the little gray spider!

You see, the spiders lived in the corners of the sunny attic and the dark corners of the nice cellar. And they were expecting to see the Christmas Tree as much as anybody. But just before Christmas a great cleaning-up began in the house. The house-mother came sweeping and dusting and wiping and scrubbing, to make everything grand and clean for the Christ child's birthday. Her broom went into all the corners, poke, poke—and of course the spiders had to run. Dear, dear, how the spiders had to run! Not one could stay in the house while the Christmas cleanness lasted. So, you see, they couldn't see the Christmas tree.

Spiders like to know all about everything, and see all there is to see, and they were very sad. So at last they went to the Christ child and told him all about it.

"All the others see the Christmas tree, dear Christ child," they said, "but we, who are so domestic and so fond of beautiful things, we are cleaned up! We cannot see it at all."

The Christ child was very sorry for the little spiders when he heard this, and he said they should see the Christmas tree.

The day before Christmas when nobody was noticing, he let them all go in, to look as long as ever they liked.

They came creepy, creepy, down the attic stairs, creepy, creepy, up the cellar stairs, creepy, creepy, along the halls—and into the beautiful room. The fat mother spiders and the old papa spiders were there, and all the little teenty, tonty, curly spiders, the baby ones. And then they looked! Round and round the tree they crawled, and looked and looked and looked. Oh, what a good time they had! They thought it was perfectly beautiful. And when they looked at everything they could see from the floor, they started up the tree to see some more. All over the tree they ran, creepy, crawly, looking at every single thing. Up and down, in and out, over every branch and twig the little spiders ran, and saw every one of the pretty things right up close.

They stayed until they had seen all there was to see, you may be sure, and then they went away at last, quite happy.

Then, in the still, dark night before Christmas Day, the dear Christ child came, to bless the tree for the children. But when he looked at it—what do you suppose?—it was covered with cobwebs! Everywhere the little spiders had been they had left a spiderweb; and you know they had been just everywhere. So the tree was covered from its trunk to its tip with spiderwebs, all hanging from the branches and looped around the twigs; it was a strange sight.

What could the Christ child do? He knew that house-mothers do not like cobwebs; it would never, never do to have a Christmas Tree covered with those. No, indeed.

So the dear Christ child touched the spiders' webs, and turned them all to gold! Wasn't that a lovely trimming? They shone and shone, all over the beautiful tree. And that is the way the Christmas tree came to have golden cobwebs on it.

SONG FROM HEAVEN

BY HERTHA PAULI

On the 24th of December, 1818, in Hallein, an age-old village in the Austrian Alps, Father Joseph Mohr sat alone in his study, reading the Bible. All through the valley the children were filled with excitement, for it was Holy Eve, and they could stay up for Midnight Mass. On their way down the open, frozen trails they carried rushlights, so that from the village the valley looked like a huge Christmas tree with a hundred moving candles.

The young priest had no eyes for the valley that was so festively lighted. With open Bible, he sat at his oaken study table working on a sermon for the midnight service. He read again the story of the shepherds in the fields to whom the angel came and said: "Unto you is born this day in the City of David a Savior . . ."

Just as Father Mohr read this passage a knock sounded at his door. He admitted a peasant woman wrapped in a coarse shawl, who told him of a child born earlier that day to a poor charcoal-maker's wife living on one of the highest alps in his parish. The parents had sent her to ask the priest to come and bless the infant, that it might live and prosper.

Father Mohr was strangely moved on his visit to the poorly lighted ramshackle hut where the young mother lay on the crude bed smiling happily, with her baby asleep in her arms. The scene did not resemble the manger in the City of David, yet the last words he had read in his Bible suddenly seemed to be addressed to him. When he returned to the valley, he saw that the dark slopes were alight with the torches of the mountaineers on their way to church, and from all the villages far and near, bells began to ring.

To Father Mohr a true Christmas miracle had come to pass. Sitting in his study after the midnight service, he tried to put down on paper what had happened to him. The words kept turning into verse, and when dawn broke, Father Mohr had written a poem. And on Christmas Day his friend, Franz Xavier Gruber, music teacher in the village school, composed music to fit the verses.

Village children heard the priest and the teacher singing. The church organ was out of order so the pair were using what they had—two voices and a guitar, which Franz Gruber played. "The Lord can hear us without an organ," Gruber said.

They did not know that this anniversary of Christ's birthday was also the birthday of a great Christmas hymn that would be known in all lands where there is a Christmas, and that four little children would one day start it on its way to fame.

Of all the youngsters in the Zillertal Valley in the Austrian Tyrol, the ones with the most beautiful voices were the four Strasser children, Caroline, Joseph, Andreas, and little Amalie—who was called Maly, and was so young that she couldn't pronounce the words correctly.

"Those Strassers," the townspeople used to say, "sing just like the nightingales."

Like the nightingales too, every spring the four children traveled northward to Leipzig, in the kingdom of Saxony, the site of the great annual Trade Fair. For their parents were glove-makers, and it was the children's chore to display and sell the soft chamois gloves that were sought far and wide.

Leipzig, at Fair time, was an exciting city, and the youngsters from the Zillertal at times felt lost in the bright and curious crowd. But they did just what they did at home when their spirits needed lifting—they sang together. The song they sang most, because it was their favorite, was "Song from Heaven."

Karl Mauracher, far-famed Zillertal organ-builder, had taught the children the song. Once he had been called to a neighborhood village to repair an organ, and when his work was done, he had asked the organist to try it out. The organist was Franz Gruber, and somehow he slipped into the Christmas melody he had composed for Father Mohr.

"I never heard that song before," the organ-builder said with awe in his voice. "Would you mind if I took it with me? Folks back where I live would appreciate it." Gruber had offered to write it down, but Mauracher told him that he knew hundreds of songs, and one more would make no difference.

The song quickly became popular in his valley, and was called "Song from Heaven." The organ builder didn't realize that he had brought back a truly valuable gift from two composers unknown to the entire world.

The children found the song's charm worked in the busy city; passersby stopped to listen and were enchanted by the beautiful, melodious tune. One day an elderly gentleman, who introduced himself as Mr. Phlenz, Director General of Music in the kingdom of Saxony, gave them tickets to one of the concerts that he conducted regularly in the *Gewandhaus*, the ancient guild house of the drapers of Leipzig. The youngsters were delighted.

When they entered the brilliantly lighted auditorium filled with silk-hatted gentlemen and ladies in rustling gowns, they felt timid and were glad to be led to inconspicuous seats beneath the platform. They were still rapt and glowing at the concert's end, when the shock came. For Mr. Pohlenz rose to announce that there were four children present with the finest voices he had heard in years. They might be persuaded to treat Their Royal Majesties, the King and Queen of Saxony, who were present, and the audience, to some of their lovely Tyrolean airs.

The announcement took the youngsters' breath away, and their faces flamed as people began to applaud. "Let's just shut our eyes and pretend we're singing at home," Maly whispered to the others.

Their first song was "Song from Heaven," and when they had finished it, there was a moment of almost reverent quiet before applause broke loose. They sang all the songs they knew, and when they knew no more, they sang "Song from Heaven" again.

The audience was still shouting for more when a gentlemen in uniform came up on the platform and said that Their Majesties desired to receive the singers.

"That was very pretty indeed," the King said after the children had been introduced. "We've never heard that Christmas song before. What is it?"

"It is a Tyrolean folk song, Your Highness," said Joseph.

"Won't you come to the castle and sing it on Christmas?" the Queen asked. "Our children will love it."

So it happened that on Holy Eve of the year 1832, in the Royal Saxon Court Chapel in Pleissenburg Castle, the Strasser children sang at the end of the Christmas services:

"Silent night! holy night!

All is calm, all is bright,
Round yon Virgin Mother and Child!
Holy Infant, so tender and mild,
Sleep in heavenly peace,
Sleep in heavenly peace."

And on that Christmas Eve the song bade the children farewell, to spread quietly around the world.

For years, on each Holy Eve, "Silent Night" was sung in the village of Hallein, in the house where Gruber lived and died, by a choir accompanied by Gruber's grandson, who used his grandfather's original guitar in the accompaniment. Later this yearly performance was carried round the world by radio—until a day in 1938 when the land of Austria was wiped off the map, and the little song of peace became "undesirable."

But the great land of music from which it hails knows no frontiers. And the "Song from Heaven," like the Christmas message itself, still rings for all men of goodwill, and has since found its way again into the country where it was born.

SILENT NIGHT
Joseph Mohr and Franz Gruber

Silent Night, holy night!
All is calm, all is bright
Round yon Virgin Mother and Child!
Holy Infant, so tender and mild,
Sleep in heavenly peace,
Sleep in heavenly peace.

Silent night, holy night!
Shepherds quake at the sight!
Glories stream from heaven afar!
Heav'nly Hosts sing allelluia!
Christ the Savior is born!
Christ the Savior is born!

A CHRISTMAS CAROL
Martin Luther

Ah! dearest Jesus, Holy Child,
Make Thee a bed, soft, undefil'd
Within my heart, that it may be
A quiet chamber kept for Thee.
My heart for very joy doth leap,
My lips no more can silence keep,
I too must sing, with joyful tongue,
That sweetest ancient cradle song,
   Glory to God in highest Heaven,
   Who unto man His Son hath
   given.
While angels sing, with pious mirth,
A glad New Year to all the earth.

PFEFFERNÜSSE
(PEPPERNUT COOKIES)

2 eggs, *lightly beaten*
1 cup of sugar
¼ cup almonds, *ground*
¼ cup candied orange peel and citron,
   chopped
¼ teaspoon cloves
½ teaspoon ground ginger

1 teaspoon cinnamon
¼ teaspoon ground pepper
the grated rind of 1 lemon
3 cups of flour, *sifted*
¼ cup, rum
confectioner's sugar

Beat the eggs and the sugar until foamy; then add the almonds and candied fruits to the egg mixture. Put flour into a separate bowl, and add the spices and lemon rind, mixing well. Slowly combine egg mixture and flour mixture. Knead dough until firm and shiny, forming the dough into a long roll, roughly 1½ inches thick. Chill until firm, and cut into ½ inch slices.

Place dough on greased baking sheets, and let stand overnight uncovered. Turn each over on the sheet, and bake for 20 minutes in a 300 degree oven, or until lightly browned. While still warm, sprinkle with rum and confectioner's sugar. Store in an airtight container.

MAKES APPROXIMATELY 50 "NUTS"

RHEINISCHER WEIHNACHTSSALAT
RHENISH CHRISTMAS SALAD

¼ pound roast veal
¼ pound salami
1 large herring, *filleted*
1 cup cooked apples
2 cups cooked potatoes
3 gherkins, *sliced*
mayonnaise, *preferably homemade, to*
   taste

½ cup milk
½ cup meat broth
10 walnuts, *chopped*
10 hazelnuts, *chopped*
2 hard-boiled eggs, *sliced*
parsley for garnish

Thinly slice meats and fish, and cube apples and potatoes. Add liquids, tossing gently, then add nuts. Serve garnished with parsley.

LESLIE'S GRANDMOTHER'S *SPAETZLE*
(DUMPLINGS)

4   large eggs
1½ cups water
¼   teaspoon nutmeg
salt and pepper to taste

3   cups flour
4   tablespoons butter
¾   cup unseasoned bread crumbs
    (preferably homemade)

Place eggs in mixing bowl; add water, nutmeg, salt, and pepper. Fold in flour with a rubber spatula, and mix well. Bring a large quantity of water to boil. Place a small amount of batter on a cutting board and, using a knife, push small slivers of the batter into the boiling water. As soon as the dumplings rise to the top, remove with a slotted spoon and drain. Continue in the same way with the remaining batter. Then melt butter in a skillet and sauté the bread crumbs until golden. Add the dumplings and toss to heat through. Serve immediately.

SERVES 8 TO 12

CHRISTMAS GOOSE WITH FRUIT

1   12 pound goose
2½ cups cooked apples
2   cups raisins, soaked in water or
    rum
2   cups dried apricots
2   cups prunes, soaked in water to
    soften

3   pears, cut into cubes
1   teaspoon ginger
1   teaspoon cinnamon
½   teaspoon freshly ground nutmeg
4   cloves
sweet wine for basting

Preheat the oven to 350 degrees. Prick the goose all over so that the fat can run out during cooking. Rub lemon juice and salt and pepper over the skin; sprinkle the bird's cavities with salt. Meantime lightly mix all the stuffing ingredients, using both the fruits and the soaking liquids. Stuff and truss the goose. There should be no need to baste the goose until the last hour of cooking; a 12-pound goose takes approximately 3 hours and 20 minutes to roast; the meat thermometer should read 180 degrees.

CHRISTSSTOLLEN
(DRESDEN *STOLLEN*)

2	cups raisins
4	ounces currants
4	ounces candied lemon peel, chopped
4	ounces candied orange peel, chopped
1	cup almonds, sliced
2	jiggers of rum
7½	cups of flour

4	ounces yeast
1½	cups sugar
1	cup plus 1 teaspoon milk, at room temperature
1½	cups butter, softened
½	cup butter, melted (for brushing loaf)
confectioner's sugar	

Pour rum over the first five ingredients, and let stand overnight covered. Crumble the yeast into the milk, then add to the flour together with the butter and sugar. Knead into a smooth dough. Cover, and leave to rise in a warm place for 20 minutes. Then add the ingredients steeped in rum to the dough, and knead thoroughly. Let the dough rise for another 30 minutes, covered. Knead again, then roll out onto a lightly floured surface to make an oval slab about 1¼ inch thick. Using a rolling pain, make a groove down the center of the dough, and then fold one half over the other half. Let rise again, this time in a greased baking pan, for 15 minutes.

Preheat the oven to 400 degrees, and bake for 20 minutes. Then lower oven temperature to 350 degrees, and bake an additional 70 minutes. If *stollen* browns too quickly, cover with tin foil.

After baking, brush with melted butter and spread on sugar thickly while still warm.

POLAND

The stars that shine in the winter sky over Poland illuminate the American night as well, and symbolically unite the two countries during the Christmas season. For the star is the dominant symbol of the Polish Christmas, from the evening star that signals the start of the Christmas Eve feast to the stars of silver and straw that sparkle on the boughs of Polish Christmas trees.

As in other European countries, St. Nicholas comes bearing gifts on the sixth of December. But for Poles from Krakow to Chicago, the real holiday is Christmas Eve, or *Wigilia* (also known as the Festival of the Star). The gleam of the first evening star means that the day's fast will soon be ended. And end it does, in a meal that can sometimes last for hours and is always charged with symbolism. Bits of straw are placed beneath the table to recall the manger at Bethlehem, and an empty plate and chair are set out for the Christ child. (In some families other empty plates bring to mind absent friends and relatives.) The meal begins with the breaking of the *oplatek*, a thin wafer stamped with scenes from the Bible. The ceremony, which derives from the sharing of the Host at Holy Communion, represents friendship and peace and also recalls, of course, the breaking of bread at the Last Supper. It is so central

to the Polish celebration of Christmas that *oplatki* are often sent to faraway family members during Advent (many an *oplatek* having made its perilous way through the international mails from Poland to America). Traditionally, both the wafers and the food to follow were blessed by a visiting priest (or taken in baskets to the local church).

After this solemn ceremony a festive mood prevails, as the feasting begins with a meal of twelve courses to represent the twelve Apostles; this always includes some kind of fish (pike with saffron, perhaps, or carp with raisins and honey), as meat is forbidden until Christmas Day. Traditional accompaniments are beet soup, noodles with poppy seeds, buckwheat groats, dumplings filled with sauerkraut, meatless *bigos* (savory stuffed pastries), poppyseed wafers, the fruit jelly known as *kisiel,* cookies, cakes, nuts, and dried and fresh fruits. After supper the Star Man (the village priest, in the Polish countryside, or a well-disguised neighbor or family member when no priest is available) arrives to quiz the children on questions of religion. He distributes modest gifts to those well versed in the catechism and reprimands those perhaps too taken with the secular aspects of the season. Customarily he is accompanied by his helpers, the Star Boys, who in turn are joined by neighborhood children dressed as animals or characters of the Nativity. After the quizzing and gift-giving, the Star Boys and animals sing carols (known as *koledy*) for gifts of their own.

Christmas Eve ends with *Pasterka,* also known as the Shepherd's Mass, celebrated at midnight both in Poland and in the United States, when the churches are awash in light and the tang of pine

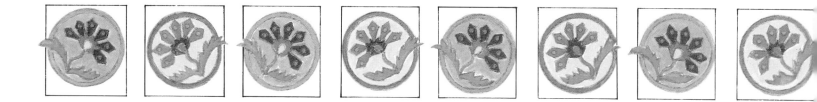

needles scents the air. Each church features an elaborate crèche, either close to the altar or just outside the entryway.

The week between Christmas and New Year's Day is especially festive in Polish communities, for this is the time of the *szopka*, the traditional puppet shows that depict Christ's birth and scenes from his life. Like most Christmas pageants, they had their beginnings in the passion plays of the Middle Ages. By the fourteenth century, however, the living players had been replaced by puppets, and four hundred years later the puppet shows were as secular as they were religious, including scenes from everyday Polish life and featuring peasants, soldiers, beggars, and shopkeepers. The *szopka* of Krakow were particularly grand, elaborately decorated with tinsel and candles, though the typical *szopka* today is likely to be a cardboard box painted to resemble a stable or a Gothic church.

The Polish Christmas lasts until Epiphany, when in many communities the Star Man returns for a final visit. He is the last reminder of the star of Bethlehem until the pageant begins anew under the stars of yet another Christmas season.

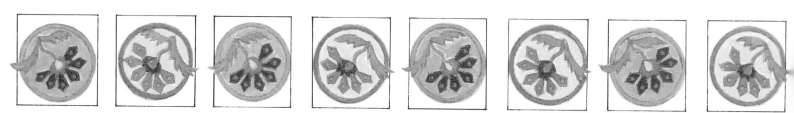

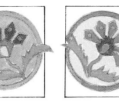

JESUS CHRIST IS BORN
Traditional Polish Carol

Jesus Christ is born
Now unto the world.
Every dark of night
Turned into light.
Hosts of angels, hear them singing
Hymns of joy, and praises ringing:
Gloria, gloria, gloria in excelsis Deo!

In the fields the shepherds
By their flocks abiding,
Harkened to the angel:
Hear yet this great tiding!
Go ye, go to Bethlehem yonder,
There to see salvation's wonder:
Gloria, gloria, gloria in excelsis Deo!

CHRISTMAS LULLABY
Traditional Polish Carol

Hush-a-bye, Baby, my heart's loveliest
treasure,
Hush-a-bye, Jesus, sweet beyond
measure,
Hush, and Thy mother will sooth all
thy sorrow,
Baby will smile on us all of tomorrow.

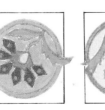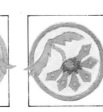

THE GENTLE BEASTS

Traditional Polish Carol

The gentle beasts of field and fold
On Christmas Eve, so bleak and cold,
At midnight all, with one accord
Kneel to adore their newborn Lord.

And then to one another tell
The story that they know so well;
The tale of that first Christmas morn
When angels sang, "The Christ is
born!"

CAROL OF THE HAY

Traditional Polish Carol

Mary, the Maiden,
When she bore dear Jesus,
Tenderly laid Him
Where the hay was sweetest.

Fresh hay,
O fresh hay,
Fragrant as the lily!

You are the cradle
For the Son of Mary.

142

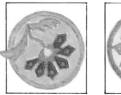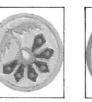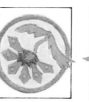

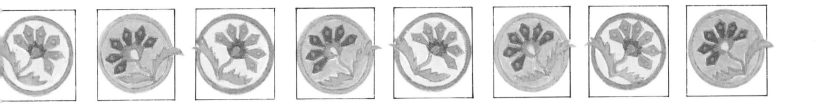

RED CABBAGE WITH MUSHROOMS

1 head red cabbage
2 tablespoons butter
1 medium onion, finely chopped

2½ cups mushrooms, sliced
2   teaspoons caraway seeds
3   tablespoons sour cream

Cut the cabbage in quarters and steam for 15 to 20 minutes, or until soft. Melt the butter and in it sauté the onion until transparent; add the mushrooms and sauté until just soft, about 5 minutes. Add cabbage and caraway seeds and heat through, stirring well. Stir in sour cream and serve either hot or cold.

BABKA

4   packages yeast
1   teaspoon salt
½   cup granulated sugar
4   eggs
1   teaspoon vanilla
4½ cups flour

½ cup butter
1 cup sultanas
½ cup candied cherries, chopped
⅓ cup brandy or rum
3 tablespoons whipping cream
1 cup confectioner's sugar

In one cup of water at room temperature, dissolve the yeast and add the salt and sugar. Stir in eggs and vanilla and enough flour to make the mixture doughy. Soften the butter and add to dough. If necessary, add additional flour. Flour a pastry board and knead dough for about ten minutes, until it is quite pliable. Place in a lightly floured bowl and cover with a dish towel. Place in a cool place and let rise for half an hour. Punch the dough down and knead again, for about five minutes. After dough has been allowed to double in bulk, punch down again and add sultanas and cherries. Place dough in a greased 10-inch pan and allow to rise until doubled in size. Bake in a preheated 375-degree oven for 45 minutes. Place on a decorative platter and sprinkle with liquor. Mix cream, at room temperature or slightly warmer, with sugar to form an icing and brush on *babka*.

143

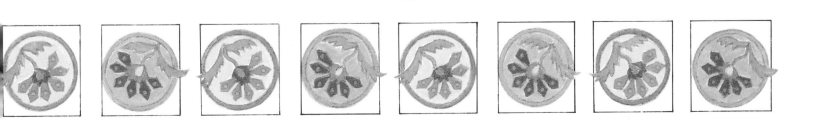

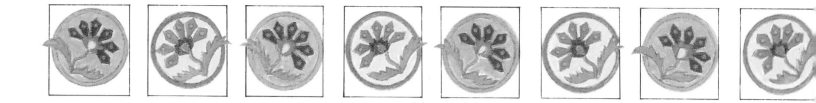

POPPY SEED CAKE

3 eggs
½ cup granulated sugar
½ cup finely chopped hazelnuts
½ cup candied orange peel, chopped

½ cup raisins
½ cup dried apricots, chopped
⅓ cup flour
½ cup ground poppy seeds

Beat the eggs until fluffy and add the sugar, nuts, and fruit. Sift the flour twice, then fold into batter with poppy seeds. Lightly butter an 8-inch cake pan and bake in a pre-heated 375-degree oven for 45 minutes, or until a toothpick inserted in the center of the cake comes out dry. The cake can be topped with chocolate icing if desired.

PIERNIKI

4 eggs
1 cup sugar
peel of 1 orange, finely grated
1 cup ground almonds
⅓ cup fresh orange juice

1 teaspoon vanilla
¼ teaspoon ground cloves
¼ teaspoon cinnamon
⅓ cup candied citron, chopped fine

Beat the eggs until foamy and add sugar. Add remaining ingredients and mix well. Line a cookie sheet with foil so that the foil forms an edge about one-inch high and line with wax paper. Spread the mixture over this and bake in a pre-heated 375-degree oven for 30 minutes or until a toothpick inserted in the center comes out dry. Cut into four-inch portions and let cool.

ICING

1 cup confectioner's sugar
1 egg white

2 teaspoons lemon juice

Mix together until thickened and spread over each serving of cooled pastry.

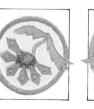

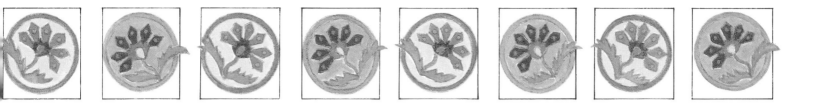

IN CLEAN HAY
ERIC P. KELLY

In a little village on the outskirts of the Polish city of Krakow there stands a happy farmhouse whose owner is Pan Jan. In the early spring the fields about the house are dark and rich, awaiting the planting of seed; and in the summer they are green with ripened grain. In the fall they turn to russet brown; and in the winter they lie deep beneath the shining snow. From earliest morning until sundown the house is astir with action, but at sundown everything ceases and peace descends, for did the Lord not ordain that all work should cease with the sun? Then the lamp is lighted in the large room and the newspaper which has come from Krakow will be read to all the family by the father or the eldest boy, Antek. The others sit about and listen. Antek is fifteen and goes every day to the high school in the city; it is a walk of about three miles, but the road is good and there is often company on the way.

Antek reads from the gazette: "Tomorrow is the day before Christmas and there will be many visitors who come to the city to attend services at night in the churches. The Christmas trees will be on sale in the Rynek (market place) and the booths full of candy and toys will be opened directly after dark. In the homes, the children will await the sight of the first star: when the first star shines, then an angel will come and knock at the door, and the rejoicing at the birth of Christ will begin. This year there will be a special treat for Krakow people, for a very famous performer will give his puppet play, the Szopka Krakowska, at the Falcon Hall on Grodska Street. With him will be his wife, who will sing the hymns."

Antek put down the paper, "Our puppet show is all made."

The father: "Don't stay out too late."

Antek answered quickly: "No, little Father, we won't. We will give our show several times betwen five and seven o'clock and then we will start on the road home."

In one corner of the little farmhouse stood a small, wooden two-towered church in miniature; between the towers at the base, large doors stood wide open, revealing a stage. And on this stage were piled a number of little wooden figures, like dolls, dressed in various jaunty colors, and in the background was the figure of a woman with a baby in her arms. This was a stage in miniature—a Szopka Krakowska with its little wooden puppets. When set up for the entertainment of lookers-on,

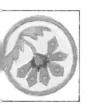
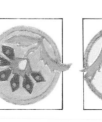

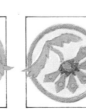

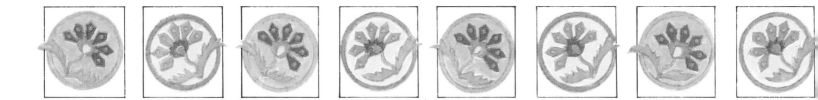

Antek would crawl beneath it and operate the puppets from little sticks that went through a slot in the floor. This slot extended the whole length of the stage, so that a puppet could be brought upon the scene from one side, made to perform, and then be taken away on the farther side. During the performance of a puppet play the figures moved in constant succession across the stage.

The mother entered from the stove room with a huge pot of steaming soup and poured it out into wooden bowls before each of the children.

"Well, tomorrow will be Christmas Eve," she said, "and you will go out with the Szopka."

"Yes. And make a lot of money." This was from Stefan, the second in age. He was a more practical boy than his brother, although younger—yet he had less of the vivid imagination which made Antek the better showman of the puppet show.

The mother sighed. "I wish we could give it to you; but what we have is being laid by against the days when you go up to the university. How much did you make last year?"

"Fifty zlotys (about five dollars)," answered Antek proudly.

"We'll make a hundred this year," said Stefan.

"And what will you do with it?"

asked the mother.

A clamor went up. Antek was saying something about a book, Stefan about a chest of tools, and Anusia, the "baby" of ten years, said something that sounded like "shoes." Christopher, who played all the songs for the Szopka on his violin, tried to make known his want for new strings and a bow. However, the whole pandemonium was such that any one might see that at least *something* was wanted rather eagerly: it was true, as the mother had said, that the scanty profits from the farm were going into the children's educations: Antek for the university, Stefan for the school of commerce and trade, Christopher for the academy of music, and Anusia—for—well, that would come later. The child had a clear and appealing voice, and might become a great singer if placed with the proper teachers. Who knows?

Therefore this chance for making a little money on the night before Christmas meant a great deal to them all. The boys, working with the father, had built the little theatre themselves. It stood upon little folding legs which Stefan had devised. The mother had dressed the dolls, and on the night before Christmas it was all in readiness to carry to Krakow. Now, since the very earliest days of the city, boys have gone about in Krakow giving this

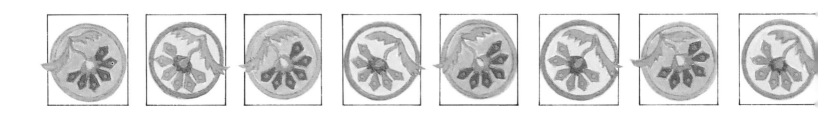

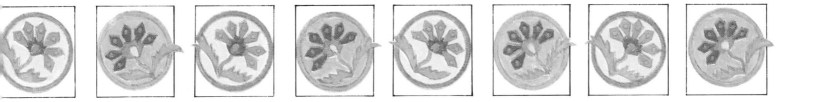

show on Christmas Eve, most of them poor or needy boys to whom the gift of money was a veritable godsend. And on Christmas Eve there descends over the earth, each year, that spirit of gladness and kindness that makes people eager and anxious to relieve suffering and soften the hard ways of life with the cheer that the Christ child brought to men.

The day before Christmas dawned bright. It was crisp but not so cold as usual. There was not a cloud in the sky, and the children knew that they could not have selected a better day for their puppet show. At about one o'clock in the afternoon they started for Krakow. Antek walked in front with the Szopka strapped on his shoulders. Stefan, carrying the sticks on which the Szopka was to rest, walked by his side. Christopher on the left side, carrying his violin and bow in a case in one hand, had extended the other hand to Anusia, who walked just beyond. A happy company it was, and all along the way people greeted them and shouted out "Wesolych Swiat" (Merry Christmas!) or else "Niech bendzie pochwalony Jesus Christ." (May Jesus Christ be praised.) As they neared the city the sun was sinking, for they had walked slowly and, too, the sun sinks early in the Christmas season. Lights were coming on everywhere, and as they stood

at the Florian Gate, Anusia turning about screamed with delight and pointed at the sky.

For there, hanging like a little candle, was the first star. The Christmas season had begun.

In the market place they selected a corner by one path and mounted the puppet theatre on its legs. "It was here that we stood last year," said Antek.

Candles were lighted before the little theatre; a crowd gathered. Then Anusia stepped out before the people, and bravely sang a little carol, while Christopher played on the violin. The crowd increased.

"Oh, what a crowd!" cried Stefan, rubbing his hands. "Here at least for the first performance is a good twenty-five zlotys." His words were correct. The first performance netted exactly that amount. It was a splendid performance too: Anusia sang the carols beautifully, Antek made the puppets dance as if they were alive, and everybody reached for handkerchiefs when King Herod ordered that all the babies in the kingdom should be put to death.

They had begun again when suddenly there came a rude end to their performance, and to all their hopes.

A dignitary wearing a huge star stepped into the circle before the little theatre and ordered the play to be stopped.

"We can't! We can't!" shrieked

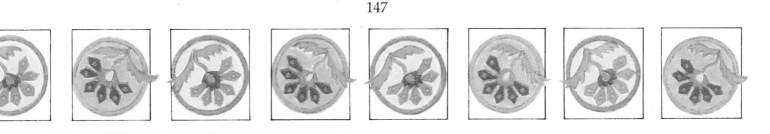

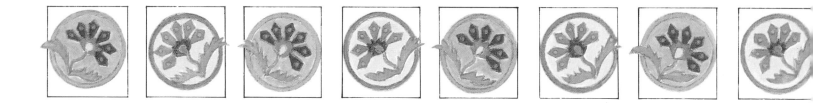

Stefan, who was reading the lines for the puppets. "Don't bother us. The show must go on."

The dignitary grinned. "Where is your license?" he asked.

"License?" Antek crept out from beneath the threatre where he was operating the puppets and faced the officer.

"Yes. Don't you know that you must buy a license to give public performances in this city?"

"No. It was not so last year."

"But it is so this year. It is a new ordinance that no shows may be given on the streets without a license."

"How much is the license?" asked Antek.

"One hundred zlotys," said the man.

"But I haven't got one hundred zlotys!"

"Then you must move along or I will report you to the police." He motioned to a police officer on the corner.

"Come quick," ordered Antek, snatching up the theatre to his back. "Take the stool, Stefan, and you, Anusia, hang on to Christopher."

They emerged in a quiet place behind the Cloth Hall to take counsel.

"We can't do anything. We've got to go home," Antek announced. Every face fell. Anusia began to cry. "It can't be helped. We must obey the law and we haven't one hundred

zlotys in the world."

"Let's give the show in some private street," suggested Stefan.

"Can't be done. We'd be arrested."

They marched out into the street. Two men engaged in a spirited conversation almost ran them down.

"Look out there," said one, sidestepping the Szopka. "The street doesn't belong to you boys."

"No, but we have our rights," answered Antek.

"That you have," answered the second man suddenly striking Antek in friendly fashion upon the back. "A Szopka, as I live!"

"A Szopka—" the second man fell back in amazement.

"Yes, and a good one," said the first man examining the show quickly. "Here is an answer to our prayers sent from Heaven. Do you people operate the Szopka?"

"We do," answered Antek wonderingly.

"Do you want an engagement?"

"Yes!" shouted Antek, Stefan, and Christopher at the tops of their voices.

"Then come with us. You see, we were to have had a very famous Szopka with us tonight—Pan Kowalski and his wife were to entertain us. The crowd is all there—has been for half an hour—waiting for the show to begin. And there is no Pan Kowalski. We have looked up

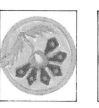

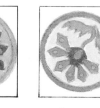

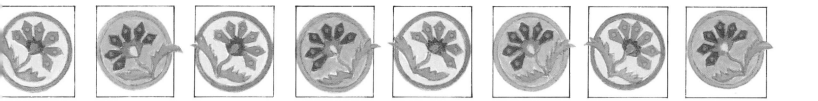

and down the town; we have hunted all through the villages, we have inquired everywhere that he might have been, and yet we cannot find him. We must have the show or send the people home."

"How much do we get?" asked Stefan, characteristically, for he had recovered from his astonishment at this quick turn of affairs.

"We will take a collection. We can at least guarantee you one hundred zlotys. You will probably make much more than that."

As they spoke the two men hustled the children along Grodska Street and stopped in front of a building on which there was a coat of arms bearing the figure of a falcon.

"In here," said one of the men.

"Why this is the Falcon Hall we read of in the newspaper," said Stefan. "This is the best place in the Krakow in which to give the Szopka. Antek, do you realize"—he turned to his brother, "that we will make lots of money out of this?"

"We must give a good performance first," admonished Antek.

One of the men made a speech to the people, while the children prepared the show. He was sorry, he said, that Pan Kowalski had not been able to come. But in his place there had come a very fine Szopka operated by young men who were quite experienced—at this the crowd laughed, for the youth of the performers was quite evident. "It is Christmas Eve," the man went on. "And it is not the time to show any displeasure. We have come here to see acted the old story of the wonderful evening so many centuries ago when Christ was born to earth to bring peace and good will to all men."

It was a Christmas crowd at that, and if it felt any ill will at this substitution on the program, it did not show it. The lamp in front of the stage was lighted. Antek stepped out in front and played on his little bugle the Heynal, or little trumpet song that the trumpeter in the tower of the Church of Our Lady had played every hour of the day and night since Christianity in Krakow began. Then lights appeared in the two towers, and Christopher and Anusia stepped out to play and sing the old hymn, "Amid the Silence." The curtains were swept back by Stefan, and there on the stage were two shepherds sleeping. Red fire is burned, an angel descends, and again Christopher and Anusia step forward. This time the song is "Gloria in Excelsis," the song sung by the angels when Christ was born. The curtain is closed. It opens again on Bethlehem, whither the shepherds have come to greet the Christ child, who lies there with the Mother, asleep on the clean hay.

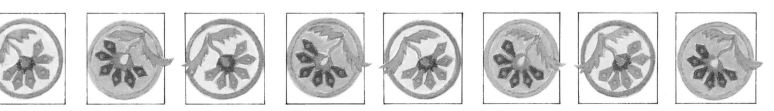

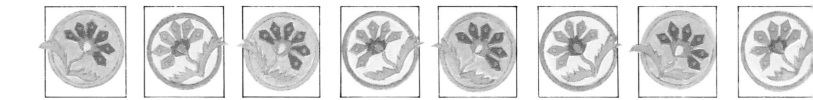

From the back of the manger a sheep and a cow look over the wall.

Then the scene changes. We are now in the court of Herod, the king, and Three Kings come in from the East to ask their way to the newborn King; Herod cannot tell them, and so they go out again and follow a star that is gleaming in the heavens; here Stefan lifts into the air a great gold star which shines with brilliance when the light falls upon it. They come to the Christ child and they too worship. Then the shepherds dance, and the soldiers sing, and the violin makes merry music for all the company. It is truly a splendid sight; the children shout, the babies crow, and the men and women clap their hands in applause.

Oh thou cruel Herod! For now he commands his Hetman to send out the soldiers and destroy the Christ child: but because they do not know who the Christ child is, they must destroy every child in the kingdom. Cruel King Herod, for this thou shalt pay—for the floor of the stage opens and the Devil dances out; how the children scream as he cuts off Herod's head, and the head goes rolling out of the little theatre and onto the floor. Then there comes more dancing and singing; little Anusia sings like an angel—the men and women take her up and the children kiss her and stroke her hands.

And when the collection is taken the bowl is heaped high with paper and silver and copper. There are at least five hundred zlotys upon the plate (about fifty dollars), the best day's work that any Szopka has ever done in Krakow. The crowd leaves slowly; the men come and take their leave of the children; the show is packed up, and the four, now beaming with happiness and delight, take again the road for the village three miles away. It is a lovely night, not over cold, but just comfortably cold, and though there is no moon, the stars are as bright as the little pin points of light in the Szopka walls. As they pass the Church of Our Lady they hear the trumpet playing the Heynal, and it makes them feel suddenly that over all the world has come this happiness at the birth of Christ.

Two hours later, on the road still, they put into the home of neighbor Kolesza for a rest. He meets them at the door with a Christmas greeting and then tells them to come to the stable for there they will find a surprise.

"I had no room for them in the house," he said. "The hay of the stable is much warmer than my floor and I have a stove here where I have heat for the animals in winter. Come and you shall see."

They entered the stable. He flashed his lantern high above his head—they looked—they drew

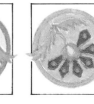

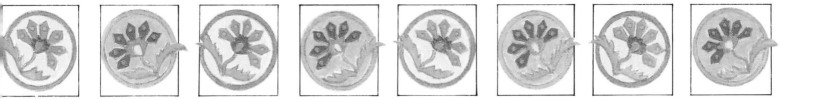

their breaths—and then with one accord fell upon their knees.

For there in the manger was a young woman. She had been sleeping but was now awake; and in her arms, nestled close to her body, was a little baby, wrapped in a blue coat.

"It is the Christ child," whispered Stefan. "See, there is the cow and the sheep looking over the back of the manger; and there is the place where the Wise Men knelt." He pointed—indeed a dark figure arose there and looked about; it was a man, and he put his fingers to his lips lest they should talk and disturb the mother and child.

"It is Pan Kowalski the puppet-show man," said Pan Kolesza in an undertone. "He was on his way to Krakow tonight to give a performance in the hall of the Falcons. He and his wife stopped here; and while they were here this child was born."

The children looked at one another strangely. Then they looked at Pan Kowalski, and then at the mother and the child.

"They have no money," went on Pan Kolesza; "they were to have received much money for their performance in Krakow tonight, but they were not able to go, and therefore they lose it. I do not know what they will do when they leave here, though the good God knows I will let them stay as long as they like. They have only this show which they give at Christmas; it is not given at any other time of the year."

"And it was on this night that Christ was born . . ." said Antek. "Stefan . . ." he added after a long pause.

"I know what you are going to say," retorted Stefan. They went out into the air again, not even taking leave of either of the men, so engrossed were they in their own thoughts.

"It means that we lose what we wanted," said Antek. "I think I'll go back."

"No," said Stefan. "Let me."

Antek squeezed something into his hand. Stefan ran back to the stable and entered. Pan Kowalski had sunk into a stupor again and heeded nothing; Stefan crept up to the manger and listened to the deep breathing of the mother. Then he slipped his hand over the edge of the manger and dropped all the silver and notes that had been collected in Krakow; then he fell upon his knees for a moment and said a little prayer. But as he staggered after his companions down the long dark road, something of the most infinite happiness seized upon his heart, and when he reached Antek he was sobbing like a baby. Whereupon Antek fell to sobbing likewise, and out there upon the Krakow road Christ was born again in the hearts of four happy children.

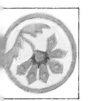

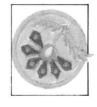

ITALY

If the American Christmas is a rich cake primarily of German and English batter, then the frosting and much of the filling is surely Italian. It was the Italians, after all, who gave us two of the most essential symbols of the season—the crèche and the Christmas carol. And the many Italian-American communities across the country celebrate the holiday with a *brio* that is nothing short of infectious.

On a midwinter's day in the small Italian town of Greccio, the villagers gathered before an unusual sight: a man and a woman, dressed as Joseph and Mary, kneeling before a cradle and surrounded by a real ox and ass who silently gave witness to the scene. This was the first crèche (*presepio* in Italian), arranged over seven hundred years ago by an Italian priest who would later be known as St. Francis of Assisi. The tradition took hold to such a dramatic degree that it soon spread to most of the Christian countries of Europe. But even today, it is especially beloved by Italians and Americans of Italian descent, many of whom erect life-size front yard *presepios* in the weeks before Christmas. Whether in the yard or a corner of the living room, the traditional *presepio* is assembled with an empty manger—to be filled with a likeness of the Christ child only on Christmas Eve.

St. Francis, too, is credited with originating the first true Christmas carols—if not by his own hand then at least by his inspiration. Many of his followers and comrades composed what one historian called "bright, homely songs on the great facts of the gospel," written not in Latin, but in so-called vulgar Italian, to be sung and enjoyed by everyone. A peculiarly Italian tradition are the shepherds' carols, originally sung by Calabrian shepherds, who came down from the hills at Advent and traveled from house to house, asking the inhabitants if Christ resided there. When the answer was yes, as it often was, they would leave behind a wooden spoon, returning later to extol the glory of the Nativity with bagpipes and song. Today the shepherds' carols are still sung in Italian homes and churches on both sides of the Atlantic, and public festivities often include a procession of the shepherds.

The Italian holiday typically begins on the first Sunday of Advent, by which time the traditional displays of *torrone*—nougat candy hard and sweet enough to represent a serious threat to the teeth—and other Christmas dainties have begun to appear in shop windows. During the *novena*—the nine-day period up to and including Christmas Day—children go from house to house, reciting Christmas verses for coins. Advent is the time, too, for the *festi Natalizie*—Christmas fairs that are anything but sedate, marked by an abundance of light and sound—the thunder and sparkle of fireworks, the crackle of bonfires, and, of course, the ubiquitous strains of holiday music.

Christmas Eve, though quieter, is also a time for lights and music. In the houses candles are lit around the *presepio,* as the Baby Jesus is passed from hand to hand and placed, to prayers and carols, in the manger. Then follows that jewel of the Italian Christmas Eve, the *pranzo della vigilia,* a meatless supper, often quite sumptuous, that always includes some variety of fish—eels, in Naples; in Sicily *baccalà* (dried, salted cod); *scungili* (squid), *calamari* (octopus), or *vongole* (clams). Christmas Eve masses begin at ten o'clock, when the streets blaze once again with torchlight and, in many cities, the reflected flash of fireworks.

Christmas Day, on the other hand, dawns quietly, the fires extinguished and the bagpipes silenced, if only temporarily. Like the French and the Spanish, the Italians reserve Christmas Day for church and family and—Italians being Italians—feasting. The Christmas dinner varies from region to region, but most often includes capon; turkey is the traditional main course in Sicily, while *zampone*—pork sausages with a sauce of lentils—is the heart of the feast in northern and central Italy. Christmas sweets include *panettone,* the traditional fruit-filled yeast cake exported in great quantities to America; *panaforte* (literally "strong bread"), and *cassata,* a kind of ice cream-and-fruit trifle. *Cuccia*—a sweet pudding of boiled wheat berries—is a Sicilian holiday treat eaten earlier in the month on Santa Lucia's Day. As in her adopted country of Sweden, where the feast of the Sicilian Santa Lucia is an intrinsic part of the Christmas season, the day commemorates the end of a great famine, during which milled wheat was unavailable.

If Christmas Day is for families, then New Year's Day is for friends, a time for parties and visiting and general holiday revelry. Though most Italian-Americans have adopted the custom of exchanging gifts on Christmas Eve or Christmas morning, New Year's is the day of gift-giving in Italy—at least for adults. The children must exercise patience—usually strained by this point—and wait until Epiphany, also known as Befana for the old woman (her name a corruption of "Epiphany") who was too busy with her cleaning to accompany the Three Kings to Bethlehem, and now roams the countryside searching for the Christ child, leaving presents in her wake. Befana's message—that we must grasp joy and love and celebration with both hands, or risk losing them forever—is fitting indeed during the joyful Italian holiday, at home and abroad.

BEFANA
TRADITIONAL FOLK TALE, RETOLD BY LESLIE GARISTO

"Comings and goings," Befana muttered as she washed down the windows. "All night and all day, nothing but comings and goings when you live on the highway to Bethlehem." Through the dripping pane the old woman could see the travelers, kicking up dust, their animals scattering straw, all of them raising too much dirt and making too much noise, even on this frigid midwinter night.

No wonder the world was in such a mess, she thought, with all this traveling and no one staying put, no one at home to keep a house tidy.

Outside a donkey brayed.

"Comings and goings," Befana grumbled, and she picked up the broom.

It would be a long night—one of the longest in a winter of long nights—but Befana would chase the hours with her broom and her dust mop till the house gleamed like a summer day. The small fire sputtered in the grate, and Befana whisked away a stray ash.

At that moment the wind rattled the door—or was it a knock? But who would be knocking at a poor old woman's door this late on a winter night? A second knock. It must be a traveler, she thought, looking for directions. Befana had no time to travel, for dusting, sweeping and polishing took all her time.

The knocking became louder still.

"Patience," Befana croaked. "I'm an old woman with too much to do. Patience!"

Cautiously she opened the door—

just a hair, to keep out the dust—but when she saw what stood on the other side her hand slipped and the door flew open. Befana stared. There stood three of the grandest travelers who'd ever graced the tired road to Bethlehem. Kingly they looked and kings they were, from the jeweled crowns on their heads to the golden slippers on their feet. But even kings could grow weary of journeying, Befana thought, noticing the mud that clung to their cloaks.

"May we enter?" the tall one asked, coughing a bit as he spoke, no doubt from the cold.

"Of course, of course," Befana said, ushering them in and all the while worrying that they would notice the unwashed walls and the new ashes that had drifted onto the hearth.

Once inside, they introduced themselves. "I am Gaspar," the tall one said, "and these" (nodding at the other two, who still stood by the door) "are Melchior and Balthazar. We are on our way to Bethlehem, to offer our gifts" (and with this he held up a bronze box, tied in ribbons of yellow silk) "to a newborn babe who will grow up to be king of all the world—a King of Peace."

"A King of Peace," Befana said, almost to herself. "Yes, that *would* be a good thing."

"A good thing indeed," said the dark one, whose name was Balthazar. "Why not come with us, then, and share in the glory of this night?"

Befana nearly agreed, until her eyes fell on the full laundry basket in the corner.

"Oh no, I couldn't. Not now," she said. "There's so much for a proper woman to do," she explained, "and never enough time to do it in."

A look of distress crossed Gaspar's face, which was quickly replaced by a polite smile. "Very well, then," he said, "but could you offer three cold and thirsty travelers something warm to drink?"

Befana ran to the hearth, where a tin pot of tea steamed. She poured out three cups and handed them shyly to her royal visitors. As they drank, she thought of the babe who would be a King of Peace. In a trunk she had a doll made of straw that had once been her own. It would make a fine gift for this newborn babe.

"Sire," she said suddenly to Gaspar, "I will join you—as soon as I've finished my work."

"Ah, that's fine," he answered. "To find us, you need only follow the star that hangs in the sky like a lamp of fire." And he gestured to the window, beyond which glowed the brightest star that Befana had ever seen.

When they had gone, the house seemed smaller, meaner, and dustier than before, so Befana set to cleaning with a fury. She washed, and dusted, and soaped, and polished till the house was as clean as a dinner plate. When the last piece of laundry

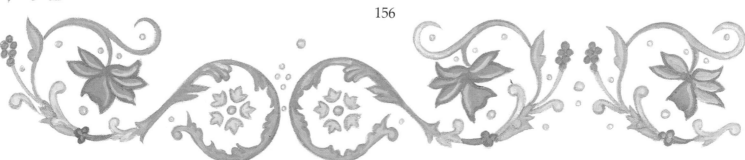

had been hung by the fire, she took the straw doll from the trunk and wrapped herself in a heavy coat. As she closed the door behind her, she turned around once to admire her good work.

But when she stood on the doorstep, she was surrounded in darkness. The night sky had clouded over, and the brilliant star had disappeared. Still she set off, hoping that the cold wind would soon blow the clouds away.

But the clouds only thickened, and a chill rain began to fall. By dawn Befana was utterly lost, her coat soaking wet, the straw doll a sodden mass in her arms. By midday she was back in her own house, so tired that not even the neat rows of crockery could cheer her.

"I'm a foolish old woman," she said aloud, "so consumed with my own work that I've missed the son of God. But perhaps I *will* find him some day," she said to cheer herself. "Yes, perhaps I will."

And so, every year at Epiphany, Befana sets out with a bagful of toys, looking for the babe in the dark midwinter night and leaving a gift with every child whose house she passes. And when she sees a woman busy at stacking straw or a man laboring over the hearth, she cries out to them, "This is a night for joy, not work! It will pass soon enough, so hold it fast!"

O COME, ALL YE FAITHFUL
(*Adeste Fideles*)

O come, all ye faithful,
Joyful and triumphant,
O come ye, O come ye to Bethlehem;
Come and behold Him,
Born the King of angels;
O come, let us adore Him,
O come, let us adore Him,
O come, let us adore Him,
Christ the Lord.

Sing, choirs of angels,
Sing in exultation
Sing, all ye citizens of heav'n above;
Glory to God
In the highest;
O come, let us adore Him,
O come, let us adore Him,
O come, let us adore Him,
Christ the Lord.

TRADITIONAL ITALIAN FOLK CAROL

On Christmas Eve,
Jesus was born
On hay and straw
And nothing else.

CAROL OF THE BAGPIPERS

A Traditional Italian Carol,
Originally in Dialect

When the Child was born at
Bethlehem,
It was night but seemed like noon,
For the brightest of the stars,
The most shining, lit the night!
That largest star
Went to call the Magi from the East.

STUFOLI
(CHRISTMAS HONEY BALLS)

4 eggs whites
1 stick butter, softened
½ cup sugar
3 cups of flour (then more, if needed)
corn oil (or other lightly flavored oil)

¼ cup honey
2 teaspoons grated orange peel
1 teaspoon vanilla extract
1 teaspoon anise liqueur
glazed fruit for topping, finely chopped,
or confectioner's sugar

Beat the first three ingredients together. Work in the flour, cup by cup, adding additional flour if necessary to make the dough stiff. Roll out onto a floured board into rolls the width of a finger; cut into 1-inch lengths. Roll between your fingers into little balls. Heat oil in a fryer; fry balls at 375 degrees for 3 minutes or until lightly browned.

Drain on paper towels, and place in a pyramid shape on a platter. Combine the honey and orange peel in a saucepan, stirring, and heat; turn off heat, add liqueur and vanilla. Pour over pyramid. The pyramid can be topped with confectioners' sugar or finely chopped glazed fruit.

PANETTONE
(Christmas fruit bread)

2 envelopes yeast
1/3 cup water
6 cups flour
2 sticks butter, softened
2 eggs, beaten
1 teaspoon lemon juice

1 tablespoon vanilla
1 tablespoon honey
3/4 cups raisins
3/4 cup glazed orange peel
3/4 cups pine nuts (pignoli)
melted butter for brushing loaves

Dissolve yeast in water. Add 1 cup of flour to the mixture, and shape dough into a ball. Let rise, in a greased bowl, covered, in a warm place for an hour. Meanwhile, mix the butter, remaining flour, eggs, sugar, vanilla, and honey; work into dough. Knead until satiny. Roll out into a rectangle, and strew raisins, peel, and nuts over dough. Fold over; then fold over again. Knead dough to distribute fruit evenly. Shape into a ball, and let rise again, covered for 30 minutes. Punch dough down; then divide into three, and form each section into a ball. Prepare a greased 8-inch round pan with a brown paper collar of three inches. Place dough in pan, and cover, let rise until doubled.

Preheat oven to 375 degrees. On top of each piece of dough, cut a cross, and brush with butter. Bake 50 minutes or until tester comes clean, brushing once or twice with melted butter during baking.

Makes three panettone

BAGNA CAUDA
(an Italian Dipping Sauce)

1 stick melted butter
1/2 cup olive oil
2 large garlic cloves, mashed

8–9 large anchovy filets, mashed
one cup scalded cream
vegetables for dipping (see below)

Simmer butter, oil, and garlic together for several minutes; add anchovies and cook until pastelike. Stir in cream and heat until hot. Serve hot in a fondue pot or chafing dish.

Among the vegetables suggested for dipping are: broccoli, green peppers, artichokes (steamed beforehand), spinach, or zucchini.

PURELY
AMERICAN

When the Pilgrims weighed anchor on the Massachusetts shore, bringing with them only a precious few belongings from the Old World, amid the cargo was a barrel of holly, ivy, and immortelles, out of which table decorations and Christmas wreaths were fashioned by some of the less doctrinaire settlers. While most of our holiday traditions have been lovingly transplanted from other climes, over the last three centuries American soil has grown its own traditions and customs, some of which are now treasured elements of Christmas in other lands.

If the stricter Puritan forefathers had had their way, we might not celebrate Christmas at all. In May 1659, the General Court of Massachusetts declared all Christmas festivities strictly illegal; revelers would be fined the then-hefty sum of five shillings. Connecticut soon followed suit. But the Dutch who had settled New

York had brought their festivities with them, along with their patron saint of sailors and merchants, St. Nicholas, whose day was celebrated on December 6th. The Dutch holiday was marked by feasting, the exchange of gifts, and brightly festooned trees (a tradition in turn borrowed from Germany). It was St. Nicholas who brought cheer and gifts to the first New Yorkers: *Sinterklass*, as he was known familiarly, or, as the English said it, *Saint Class*.

Like many an immigrant, *Sinterklass* would, after some generations, become wholly Americanized, shedding his bishop's robes and stately visage for a fur-trimmed red suit and a laughing face. Over time, even his address would change, from Spain to the North Pole. The transformation began in 1809 when Washington Irving revived him from obscurity:

Nor must I omit to record one of the earliest measures of this infant settlement {New Amsterdam}, inasmuch as it shows the piety of our forefathers, and that, like good Christians, they were always ready to serve GOD *after they had first served themselves. Thus, having quietly settled themselves down and provided for their own comfort, they bethought themselves of testifying their gratitude to the great and good St. Nicholas for his protecting care in guiding them to this delectable abode. To this end they built a fair and goodly chapel within the fort, which they consecrated to his name; whereupon he immediately took the town of New Amsterdam under his peculiar patronage, and he has ever since been and I devoutly hope will ever be, the titular saint of this excellent city. At this early period was*

instituted that pious ceremony, still religiously observed in all our ancient families of the right breed, of hanging up a stocking in the chimney on St. Nicholas eve; which stocking is always found in the morning miraculously filled—for the good St. Nicholas has ever been a great giver of gifts, particularly to children . . .—and as of yore, in the better days of man, the deities were wont to visit him on earth and bless his rural habitations, so we are told, in the sylvan days of New Amsterdam, the good St. Nicholas would often make his appearance in his beloved city, of a holiday afternoon, riding jollily among the tree tops, or over the roofs of the houses, now and then drawing forth significant presents from his breeches-pockets, and dropping them down the chimneys of his favorites. Whereas, in these degenerate days of iron and brass, he never shows us the light of his countenance, nor ever visits us, save one night in the year, when he rattles down the chimneys of the descendants of the patriarchs, confining his presents merely to the children, in token of the degeneracy of the parents.

A scant thirteen years later, in 1822, a classical scholar named Clement C. Moore wrote a poem to entertain his children which would transform the Dutch St. Nicholas forever on these shores. "A Visit from St. Nicholas" not only described a portly old man with twinkling eyes and a full white beard, but had him arriving in a flying sleigh pulled by eight reindeer! Gone forever were the white steed and the bishop's robes; even the date of St. Nick's arrival was changed, from December 6th to Christmas Eve. The poem became the most frequently reprinted Christmas verse in history, even though Moore refused to take a cent in royalties.

But it was Thomas Nast who gave Santa Claus a face we would remember. Nast, a German-born illustrator whose political caricatures for *Harper's Weekly* brought him national acclaim (he invented, among other emblems, the Democratic donkey and the Republican elephant), depicted Santa in his element, making toys, stuffing stockings, piloting his sleigh, in a series of vastly popular Christmas drawings. During the Civil War, Santa even delivered gifts to Union soldiers.

Detail by detail, *Sinterklass* became an American classic. While European children left their wooden shoes by the window or

hearth, American children—whose lace-up boots were difficult to stuff with goodies—hung up their stockings. And so, an American tradition—enshrined in countless stories and films, window displays and Coca-Cola advertisements—was born.

Often, an imported tradition became American in detail. The English brought mumming with them to these shores, with holiday enactments of the saga of St. George and the Dragon. But in the New World, St. George soon became the valiant George Washington.

Purely American, too, was the feast table with several unique dishes, most notably cranberry sauce (cranberries are indigenous to America) and the Christmas turkey. Indeed, the turkey proved so successful as a holiday entree that by the seventeenth century, it had usurped the place of the peacock in the traditional English dinner.

And that most American of preoccupations—commerce—gave the world a very American custom: Christmas shopping. Though holiday gifts had long been part of celebrations worldwide, they tended to be small tokens—cookies, candies, nuts, and dried fruits, hung on Christmas tree bough or tucked into a child's sabot. It was in nineteenth century America—in New York, to be precise—that Christmas shopping bloomed into ritual, marked by list-making, extravagance, and, of course, the exhortations of local merchants. At mid-century New York shop owners were already decking their halls and filling their windows with holly, pine, and glittering Christmas merchandise.

But perhaps nothing is as purely American as the many Native American celebrations of the season. In Arizona the Hopi *Soyal*, the winter solstice ceremony, begins with a rooftop vigil for the appearance of the dying year, represented by an old man in rags. When he is taken inside the *kiva*, the ceremonial site, the Hopis are assured once again that winter will be superseded by spring.

In New Mexico, in the shadow of the Sangre de Cristo Mountains, the Christian Indians of the Taos Pueblo call the period from December 10th through January 20th "The Time for Staying Still." The winter's quiet is broken only on Christmas Eve with a torchlight ceremony punctuated by drums and rifle shots, and on

Christmas Day with the joyous Deer Dance. Like all American observances of the season, it is a time for unbridled celebration.

Christmas in America has come a long way from that first Christmas on Plymouth Rock, eloquently described in William Bradford's diary:

1620, Plymouth Rock

Munday, the 25 Day, we went on shore, some to fell tymber, some to saw, some to rive, and some to carry, so that no man rested all that day, but towards night, some as they were at worke, heard a noyse of some Indians, which caused us all to goe to our Muskets, but we heard no further, so we came aboard againe, and left some twentie to keepe the court of gard; that night we had a sore storme of winde and raine. Munday the 25 being Christmas day, we began to drinke water aboard, but at night, the Master caused us to have some Beere, and so on board we had diverse times now and then some Beere, but on shore none at all.

On ye day called Christmas-day, ye Gov'r called them out to worke (as was used), but ye most of this new company excused themselves, and said it went against their consciences to worke on ye day. So ye Gov'r tould them that if they made it a matter of conscience, he would spare them till they were better informed. So he led away ye rest, and left them: but when they came home at noone from their worke, he found them in ye streete at play, openly; some pitching ye barr, and some at stoole ball, and such like sports. So he went to them and tooke away their implements, and told them it was against his conscience that they should play, and others worke. If they made ye keeping of it a matter of devotion, let them kepe to their houses, but there should be no gameing or revelling in ye streets. Since which time nothing hath been attempted that way, at least, openly.

Perhaps the best known affirmation of the spirit of Santa Claus was provided by Francis Church, an editorial writer for the New York *Sun.* On September 21, 1897, he responded to a letter from a troubled eight-year-old girl:

Dear Editor:

I am 8 years old. Some of my little friends say there is no Santa Claus. Papa says "If you see it in The Sun it's so." Please tell me the truth, is there a Santa Claus?

Virginia O'Hanlon,
115 West 95th Street
New York City

Little suspecting that his words would become a sort of Christmas manifesto, Church replied:

Virginia, your little friends are *wrong.* They have been affected by the skepticism of a skeptical age. They do not *believe* except they *see.* They think that nothing can be which is not comprehensible by their little minds. All minds, Virginia, whether they be men's or children's are little. In this great universe of ours man is a mere insect, an ant, in his intellect, as compared with the boundless world about him, as measured by the intelligence capable of grasping the whole of truth and knowledge.

Yes, Virginia, there *is* a Santa Claus. He exists as certainly as love, and generosity and devotion exist, and you know that they abound and give to your life its highest beauty and joy. Alas! how dreary would be the world if there were no Santa Claus! It would be as dreary as if there were no Virginias. There would be no child-like faith, then, no poetry, no romance to make tolerable this existence.

We should have no enjoyment, except in sense and sight. The Eternal light with which childhood fills the world would be extinguished.

Not believe in Santa Claus! You might as well not believe in fairies! You might get your papa to hire men to watch in all the chimneys on Christmas Eve to catch Santa Claus, but even if they did not see Santa Claus coming down what would that prove? Nobody sees Santa Claus, but that is no sign that there is no Santa Claus. The most real things in the world are those that neither children nor men can see. Did you ever see fairies dancing on the lawn? Of course not, but that's no proof that they are not there. Nobody can conceive or imagine all the wonders there are unseen and unseeable in the world.

You tear apart the baby's rattle and see what makes the noise inside, but there is a veil covering the unseen world which not the strongest man, nor even the united strength of all the strongest men that ever lived, could tear apart. Only faith, fancy, poetry, love, romance, can push aside that curtain and view—and picture the supernal beauty and glory beyond. Is it all real? Ah, Virginia, in all this world there is nothing else real and abiding.

No Santa Claus! Thank God he lives, and he lives forever. A thousand years from now, Virginia, nay, ten times ten thousand years from now, he will continue to make glad the heart of childhood.

THE BELLS
Edgar Allan Poe

Hear the sledges with the bells—
   Silver bells!
What a world of merriment their melody
   foretells!
  How they tinkle, tinkle, tinkle,
   In the icy air of night!
  While the stars, that oversprinkle
  All the heavens, seem to twinkle
   With a crystalline delight
  Keeping time, time, time,
   In a sort of Runic rhyme,
To the tintinnabulation that so
   musically wells
  From the bells, bells, bells, bells,
   Bells, bells, bells—
From the jingling and the tinkling of
  the bells.

SOMEHOW NOT ONLY FOR CHRISTMAS
John Greenleaf Whittier

Somehow not only for Christmas
  but all the long year through,
The joy that you give to others
  Is the joy that comes back to you.

And the more you spend in blessing
  The poor and lonely and sad,
The more of your heart's possessing
  Returns to make you glad.

A Visit from St. Nicholas

Clement C. Moore

'Twas the night before Christmas when
all through the house
Not a creature was stirring, not even a
mouse;
The stockings were hung by the chimney
with care,
In hopes that St. Nicholas soon would
be there;
The children were nestled all snug in
their beds
While visions of sugar plums danced in
their heads;
And Mamma in her kerchief, and I in
my cap,
Had just settled our brains for a long
winter's nap,
When out on the lawn there arose such a
clatter,
I sprang from my bed to see what was
the matter.
Away to the window I flew like a flash,
Tore open the shutter and threw up the
sash.
The moon on the breast of the new-fallen
snow
Gave a lustre of midday to objects
below,
When, what to my wondering eyes
should appear,
But a miniature sleigh and eight tiny
reindeer,
With a little old driver, so lively and
quick,

I knew in a moment it must be St.
Nick.
More rapid than eagles his coursers they
came,
And he whistled, and shouted, and
called them by name:
"Now, Dasher! now, Dancer! now,
Prancer and Vixen!
On, Comet! on, Cupid! on, Donder
and Blitzen!
To the top of the porch! to the top of the
wall!
Now dash away! dash away! dash
away, all!"
As dry leaves that before the wild
hurricane fly,
When they meet with an obstacle, mount
to the sky,
So up to the housetop the coursers they
flew,
With a sleigh full of toys, and St.
Nicholas, too.
And then, in a twinkling, I heard on
the roof
The prancing and pawing of each little
hoof.
As I drew in my head, and was
turning around,
Down the chimney St. Nicholas came
with a bound.
He was dressed all in fur, from his head
to his foot,
And his clothes were all tarnished with
ashes and soot;
A bundle of toys he had flung on his
back,
And he looked like a peddler just
opening his pack.

His eyes—how they twinkled! his
    dimples, how merry!
His cheeks were like roses, his nose like
    a cherry!
His droll little mouth was drawn up
    like a bow,
And the beard on his chin was as white
    as the snow;
The stump of a pipe he held tight in his
    teeth,
And the smoke, it encircled his head
    like a wreath;
He had a broad face and a little round
    belly
That shook, when he laughed, like a
    bowl full of jelly.
He was chubby and plump, a right jolly
    old elf,
And I laughed when I saw him, in
    spite of myself;
A wink of his eye and a twist of his
    head,
Soon gave me to know I had nothing to
    dread;
He spoke not a word, but went straight
    to his work,
And filled all the stockings; then turned
    with a jerk,
And laying a finger aside of his nose,
And giving a nod, up the chimney he
    rose.
He sprang to his sleigh, to his team
    gave a whistle,

And away they all flew like the down
    of a thistle.
But I heard him exclaim, ere he drove
    out of sight,
"Happy Christmas to all, and to all a
    good night."

O LITTLE TOWN OF BETHLEHEM
Phillips Brooks/Lewis H. Redner

O little town of Bethlehem,
How still we see thee lie.
Above thy deep and dreamless sleep
The silent stars go by;
Yet in thy dark streets shineth
The everlasting light,
The hopes and fears of all the years,
Are met in thee tonight.

For Christ is born of Mary
And gathered all above,
While mortals sleep, the angels keep
Their watch of wond'ring love.
O morning stars, together
Proclaim the holy birth,
And praises sing to God the King,
And peace to men on earth.

THE GIFT OF THE MAGI

O. HENRY

One dollar and eighty-seven cents. That was all. And sixty cents of it was in pennies. Pennies saved one and two at a time by bulldozing the grocer and the vegetable man and the butcher until one's cheeks burned with the silent imputation of parsimony that such close dealing implied. Three times Della counted it. One dollar and eighty-seven cents. And the next day would be Christmas.

There was clearly nothing to do but flop down on the shabby little couch and howl. So Della did it. Which instigates the moral reflection that life is made up of sobs, sniffles, and smiles, with sniffles predominating.

While the mistress of the home is gradually subsiding from the first stage to the second, take a look at the home. A furnished flat at $8 per week. It did not exactly beggar description, but it certainly had that word on the lookout for the mendicancy squad.

In the vestibule below was a letter-box into which no letter would go, and an electric button from which no mortal finger could coax a ring. Also appertaining thereunto was a card bearing the name "Mr. James Dillingham Young."

The "Dillingham" had been flung to the breeze during a former period of prosperity when its possessor was being paid $30 per week. Now, when the income was shrunk to $20, the letters of "Dillingham" looked blurred, as though they were thinking seriously of contracting to a modest and unassuming D. But whenever Mr. James Dillingham Young came home and reached his flat above he was called "Jim" and greatly hugged by Mrs. James Dillingham Young, already introduced to you as Della. Which is all very good.

Della finished her cry and attended to her cheeks with the powder rag. She stood by the window and looked out dully at a grey cat walking a grey fence in a grey backyard. Tomorrow would be Christmas Day, and she had only $1.87 with which to buy Jim a present. She had been saving every penny she could for months, with this result. Twenty dollars a week doesn't go far. Expenses had been greater than she had calculated. They always are. Only $1.87 to buy a present for Jim. Her Jim. Many a happy hour she had spent planning for something nice for him. Something fine and rare and sterling—something just a little bit near to being worthy of the honor of being owned by Jim.

There was a pier-glass between the windows of the room. Perhaps you have seen a pier-glass in an $8

flat. A very thin and very agile person may, by observing his reflection in a rapid sequence of longitudinal strips, obtain a fairly accurate conception of his looks. Della, being slender, had mastered the art.

Suddenly she whirled from the window and stood before the glass. Her eyes were shining brilliantly, but her face had lost its color within twenty seconds. Rapidly she pulled down her hair and let it fall to its full length.

Now, there were two possessions of the James Dillingham Youngs in which they both took a mighty pride. One was Jim's gold watch that had been his father's and grandfather's. The other was Della's hair. Had the Queen of Sheba lived in the flat across the airshaft, Della would have let her hair hang out the window some day to dry just to depreciate Her Majesty's jewels and gifts. Had King Solomon been the janitor, with all his treasures piled up in the basement, Jim would have pulled out his watch every time he passed, just to see him pluck at his beard from envy.

So now Della's beautiful hair fell about her, rippling and shining like a cascade of brown waters. It reached below her knee and made itself almost a garment for her. And then she did it up again nervously and quickly. Once she faltered for a minute and stood still while a tear or two splashed on the worn red carpet.

On went her old brown jacket; on went her old brown hat. With a whirl of skirts and with the brilliant sparkle still in her eyes, she fluttered out the door and down the stairs to the street.

Where she stopped the sign read: "Mme. Sofronie. Hair Goods of All Kinds." One flight up Della ran, and collected herself, panting. Madame, large, too white, chilly, hardly looked the "Sofronie."

"Will you buy my hair?" asked Della.

"I buy hair," said Madame. "Take yer hat off and let's have a sight at the looks of it."

Down rippled the brown cascade.

"Twenty dollars," said Madame, lifting the mass with a practised hand.

"Give it to me quick," said Della.

Oh, and the next two hours tripped by on rosy wings. Forget the hashed metaphor. She was ransacking the stores for Jim's present.

She found it at last. It surely had been made for Jim and no one else. There was no other like it in any of the stores, and she had turned all of them inside out. It was a platinum fob chain simple and chaste in design, properly proclaiming its value by substance alone and not by meretricious ornamentation—as all good things should do. It was even worthy of The Watch. As soon as she saw it she knew that it must be Jim's. It was like him. Quietness and value—the description applied to both. Twenty-one dollars they took from her for it, and she hurried home with the 87 cents. With that

chain on his watch Jim might be properly anxious about the time in any company. Grand as the watch was, he sometimes looked at it on the sly on account of the old leather strap that he used in place of a chain.

When Della reached home her intoxication gave way a little to prudence and reason. She got out her curling irons and lighted the gas and went to work repairing the ravages made by generosity added to love. Which is always a tremendous task, dear friends—a mammoth task.

Within forty minutes her head was covered with tiny, close-lying curls that made her look wonderfully like a truant schoolboy. She looked at her reflection in the mirror long, carefully, and critically.

"If Jim doesn't kill me," she said to herself, "before he takes a second look at me, he'll say I look like a Coney Island chorus girl. But what could I do—oh! what could I do with a dollar and eighty-seven cents?"

At 7 o'clock the coffee was made and the frying-pan was on the back of the stove hot and ready to cook the chops.

Jim was never late. Della doubled the fob chain in her hand and sat on the corner of the table near the door that he always entered. Then she heard his step on the stair away down on the first flight, and she turned white for just a moment. She had a habit of saying little silent prayers about the simplest everyday things, and now she whispered: "Please God, make him think I am still pretty."

The door opened and Jim stepped in and closed it. He looked thin and very serious. Poor fellow, he was only twenty-two—and to be burdened with a family! He needed a new overcoat and he was without gloves.

Jim stopped inside the door, as immovable as a setter at the scent of quail. His eyes were fixed upon Della, and there was an expression in them that she could not read, and it terrified her. It was not anger, nor surprise, nor disapproval, nor horror, nor any of the sentiments that she had been prepared for. He simply stared at her fixedly with that peculiar expression on his face.

Della wriggled off the table and went for him.

"Jim, darling," she cried, "don't look at me that way. I had my hair cut off and sold it because I couldn't have lived through Christmas without giving you a present. It'll grow out again—you won't mind, will you? I just had to do it. My hair grows awfully fast. Say 'Merry Christmas!' Jim, and let's be happy. You don't know what a nice—what a beautiful, nice gift I've got for you."

"You've cut off your hair?" asked Jim, laboriously, as if he had not arrived at that patent fact yet even after the hardest mental labour.

"Cut it off and sold it," said Della. "Don't you like me just as well, anyhow? I'm me without my hair, ain't I?"

Jim looked about the room curiously.

"You say your hair is gone?" he said, with an air almost of idiocy.

"You needn't look for it," said Della. "It's sold, I tell you—sold and gone, too. It's Christmas Eve, boy. Be good to me, for it went for you. Maybe the hairs of my head were numbered," she went on with a sudden serious sweetness, "but nobody could ever count my love for you. Shall I put the chops on, Jim?"

Out of his trance Jim seemed quickly to wake. He enfolded his Della. For ten seconds let us regard with discreet scrutiny some inconsequential object in the other direction. Eight dollars a week or a million a year—what is the difference? A mathematician or a wit would give you the wrong answer. The magi brought valuable gifts, but that was not among them. This dark assertion will be illuminated later on.

Jim drew a package from his overcoat pocket and threw it upon the table.

"Don't make any mistake, Dell," he said, "about me. I don't think there's anything in the way of a haircut or a shave or a shampoo that could make me like my girl any less. But if you'll unwrap that package you may see why you had me going a while at first."

White fingers and nimble tore at the string and paper. And then an ecstatic scream of joy; and then, alas! a quick feminine change to hysterical tears and wails, necessitating the immediate employment of all the comforting powers of the lord of the flat.

For there lay The Combs—the set of combs, side and back, that Della had worshipped for long in a Broadway window. Beautiful combs, pure tortoise shell, with jewelled rims— just the shade to wear in the beautiful vanished hair. They were expensive combs, she knew, and her heart had simply craved and yearned over them without the least hope of possession. And now, they were hers, but the tresses that should have adorned the coveted adornments were gone.

But she hugged them to her bosom, and at length she was able to look up with dim eyes and a smile and say: "My hair grows so fast, Jim!"

And then Della leaped up like a little singed cat and cried, "Oh, oh!"

Jim had not yet seen his beautiful present. She held it out to him eagerly upon her open palm. The dull precious metal seemed to flash with a reflection of her bright and ardent spirit.

"Isn't it a dandy, Jim? I hunted all over town to find it. You'll have to look at the time a hundred times a day now. Give me your watch. I want to see how it looks on it."

Instead of obeying, Jim tumbled down on the couch and put his hands under the back of his head and smiled.

"Dell," said he, "let's put our Christmas presents away and keep 'em a while. They're too nice to use just at present. I sold the watch to get the money to buy your combs. And now suppose you put the chops on."

The magi, as you know, were wise men—wonderfully wise men—who brought gifts to the Babe in the manger. They invented the art of giving Christmas presents. Being wise, their gifts were no doubt wise ones, possibly bearing the privilege of exchange in case of duplication. And here I have lamely related to you the uneventful chronicle of two foolish children in a flat who most unwisely sacrificed for each other the greatest treasures of their house. But in a last word to the wise of these days let it be said that of all who give gifts these two were the wisest. Of all who give and receive gifts, such as they are wisest. Everywhere they are wisest. They are the magi.

A MERRY CHRISTMAS
From Little Women
BY LOUISA MAY ALCOTT

Jo was the first to wake in the gray dawn of Christmas morning. No stockings hung at the fireplace, and for a moment she felt as much disappointed as she did long ago when her little sock fell down because it was so crammed with goodies. Then she remembered her mother's promise, and slipping her hand under her pillow, drew out a little crimson-covered book. She knew it very well, for it was that beautiful old story of the best life ever lived, and Jo felt that it was a true guidebook for any pilgrim going the long journey. She woke Meg with a "Merry Christmas" and bade her see what was under her pillow. A green-covered book appeared, with the same picture inside and a few words written by their mother, which made their one present very precious in their eyes. Presently Beth and Amy woke, to rummage and find their little books also—one dove-colored, the other blue; and all sat looking at and talking about them, while the east grew rosy with coming day.

In spite of her small vanities, Margaret had a sweet and pious nature, which unconsciously influenced her sisters, especially Jo, who loved her very tenderly and obeyed her because her advice was so gently given.

"Girls," said Meg seriously, looking from the tumbled head beside her to the two little nightcapped ones in the room beyond, "Mother wants us to read and love and mind these books, and we must begin at once. We used to be faithful about it, but since father went away and all this war trouble unsettled us, we have neglected many things. You can do as you please, but I shall keep my book on the table here and read a little every morning as soon as I wake, for I know it will do me good and help me through the day."

Then she opened her new book and began to read. Jo put her arm round her, and leaning cheek to cheek, read also, with the quiet expression so seldom seen on her restless face.

"How good Meg is! Come, Amy, let's do as they do. I'll help you with the hard words, and they'll explain things if we don't understand," whispered Beth, very much impressed by the pretty books and her sisters' example.

"I'm glad mine is blue," said Amy; and then the rooms were very still while the pages were softly turned and the winter sunshine crept in to touch the bright heads and serious faces with a Christmas greeting.

"Where is Mother?" asked Meg, as she and Jo ran down to thank her for their gifts, half an hour later.

"Goodness only knows. Some poor creeter come a-beggin', and your ma went straight off to see what was needed. There never was such a woman for givin' away vittles and drink, clothes and firin'," replied Hannah, who had lived with the family since Meg was born and was considered by them all more as a friend than a servant.

"She will be back soon, I think; so fry your cakes, and have everything ready," said Meg, looking over the presents, which were collected in a basket and kept under the sofa, ready to be produced at the proper time. "Why, where is Amy's bottle of cologne?" she added, as the little flask did not appear.

"She took it out a minute ago and went off with it to put a ribbon on it, or some such notion," replied Jo, dancing about the room to take the first stiffness out of the new army slippers.

"How nice my handkerchiefs look, don't they? Hannah washed and ironed them for me, and I marked them all myself," said Beth, looking proudly at the somewhat uneven letters which had cost her such labor.

"Bless the child! She's gone and put 'Mother' on them instead of 'M. March.' How funny!" cried Jo, taking up one.

"Isn't it right? I thought it was better to do it so, because Meg's initials are 'M.M.,' and I don't want anyone to use these but Marmee," said Beth, looking troubled.

"It's all right, dear, and a very pretty idea—quite sensible, too, for no one can ever mistake now. It will please her very much, I know," said Meg, with a frown for Jo and a smile for Beth.

"There's Mother. Hide the basket, quick!" cried Jo, as a door slammed and steps sounded in the hall.

Amy came in hastily, and looked rather abashed when she saw her sisters all waiting for her.

"Where have you been, and what are you hiding behind you?" asked Meg, surprised to see, by her hood and cloak, that lazy Amy had been out so early.

"Don't laugh at me, Jo! I didn't mean anyone should know till the time came. I only meant to change the little bottle for a big one, and I gave all my money to get it, and I'm truly trying not to be selfish any more."

As she spoke, Amy showed the handsome flask which replaced the cheap one; and looked so earnest and humble in her little effort to forget herself that Meg hugged her on the spot, and Jo pronounced her "a trump," while Beth ran to the window and picked her finest rose to ornament the stately bottle.

"You see I felt ashamed of my present after reading and talking about being good this morning, so I

ran round the corner and changed it the minute I was up: and I'm so glad, for mine is the handsomest now."

Another bang of the street door sent the basket under the sofa and the girls to the table, eager for breakfast.

"Merry Christmas, Marmee! Many of them! Thank you for our books, we read some, and mean to every day," they cried, in chorus.

"Merry Christmas, little daughters! I'm glad you began at once and hope you will keep on. But I want to say one word before we sit down. Not far away from here lies a poor woman with a little newborn baby. Six children are huddled into one bed to keep from freezing, for they have no fire. There is nothing to eat over there; and the oldest boy came to tell me they were suffering hunger and cold. My girls, will you give them your breakfast as a Christmas present?"

They were all unusually hungry, having waited nearly an hour, and for a minute no one spoke; only a minute, for Jo exclaimed impetuously, "I'm so glad you came before we began!"

"May I go and help carry the things to the poor little children?" asked Beth eagerly.

"I shall take the cream and the muffins," added Amy, heroically giving up the articles she most liked.

Meg was already covering the

buckwheats, and piling the bread into one big plate.

"I thought you'd do it," said Mrs. March, smiling as if satisfied. "You shall all go and help me, and when we come back we will have bread and milk for breakfast, and make it up at dinnertime."

They were soon ready, and the procession set out. Fortunately, it was early, and they went through back streets so few people saw them, and no one laughed at the queer party.

A poor, bare, miserable room it was, with broken windows, no fire, ragged bedclothes, a sick mother, a wailing baby, and a group of pale, hungry children cuddled under one old quilt, trying to keep warm.

How the big eyes stared and the blue lips smiled as the girls went in!

"Ach, mein Gott! It is good angels come to us!" said the poor woman, crying for joy.

"Funny angels in hoods and mittens," said Jo, and set them laughing.

In a few minutes it really did seem as if kind spirits had been at work there. Hannah, who had carried wood, made a fire and stopped up the broken panes with old hats and her own cloak. Mrs. March gave the mother tea and gruel, and comforted her with promises of help, while she dressed the little baby as tenderly as if it had been her own. The girls, meantime, spread the table, set the children round the fire,

and fed them like so many hungry birds—laughing, talking, and trying to understand the funny broken English.

"Das ist gut! Die Angel-kinder!" cried the poor things as they ate and warmed their purple hands at the comfortable blaze.

The girls had never been called angel children before and thought it very agreeable, especially Jo, who had been considered a "Sancho" ever since she was born. That was a very happy breakfast, though they didn't get any of it; and when they went away, leaving comfort behind, I think there were not in all the city four merrier people than the hungry little girls who gave away their breakfasts and contented themselves with bread and milk on Christmas morning.

"That's loving our neighbor better than ourselves, and I like it," said Meg, as they set out their presents while the mother was upstairs collecting clothes for the poor Hummels.

Not a very splendid show, but there was a great deal of love done up in the few little bundles; and the tall vase of red roses, white chrysanthemums, and trailing vines, which stood in the middle, gave quite an elegant air to the table.

"She's coming! Strike up, Beth! Open the door, Amy! Three cheers for Marmee!" cried Jo, prancing about, while Meg went to conduct their mother to the seat of honor.

Beth played her gayest march, Amy threw open the door, and Meg enacted escort with great dignity. Mrs. March was both surprised and touched; and smiled with her eyes full as she examined her presents and read the little notes which accompanied them. The slippers went on at once, a new handkerchief was slipped into her pocket, well scented with Amy's cologne, the rose was fastened in her bosom, and the nice gloves were pronounced a "perfect fit."

There was a good deal of laughing and kissing and explaining, in the simple, loving fashion which makes these home festivals so pleasant at the time, so sweet to remember long afterward; and then all fell to work.

The morning charities and ceremonies took so much time that the rest of the day was devoted to preparations for the evening festivities. Being still too young to go often to the theater, and not rich enough to afford any great outlay for private performances, the girls put their wits to work and—necessity being the mother of invention—made whatever they needed. Very clever were some of their production— pasteboard guitars, antique lamps made of old-fashioned butterboats covered with silver paper, gorgeous robes of old cotton, glittering with tin spangles from a pickle factory, and armor covered with the same useful diamond-shaped bits, left in sheets when the lids of tin preserve

pots were cut out. The furniture was used to being turned topsy-turvey, and the big chamber was the scene of many innocent revels.

No gentlemen were admitted, so Jo played male parts to her heart's content and took immense satisfaction in a pair of russet-leather boots given her by a friend, who knew a lady who knew an actor. These boots, an old foil, and a slashed doublet once used by an artist for some picture, were Jo's chief treasures and appeared on all occasions. The smallness of the company made it necessary for the two principal actors to take several parts apiece; and they certainly deserved some credit for the hard work they did in learning three or four different parts, whisking in and out of various costumes, and managing the stage besides. It was excellent drill for their memories, a harmless amusement, and employed many hours which otherwise would have been idle, lonely, or spent in less profitable society.

On Christmas night, a dozen girls piled onto the bed which was the dress circle, and sat before the blue and yellow chintz curtains in a most flattering state of expectancy. There was a good deal of rustling and whispering behind the curtain, a trifle of lamp smoke, and an occasional giggle from Amy, who was apt to get hysterical in the excitement of the moment. Presently a bell sounded, the curtains flew apart, and the Operatic Tragedy began.

"A gloomy wood," according to the one playbill, was represented by a few shrubs in pots, green baize on the floor, and a cave in the distance. This cave was made with a clothes-horse for a roof, bureaus for walls; and in it was a small furnace in full blast, with a black pot on it, and an old witch bending over it. The stage was dark and the glow of the furnace had a fine effect, especially as real steam issued from the kettle when the witch took off the cover. A moment was allowed for the first thrill to subside; then Hugo, the villain, stalked in with a clanking sword at his side, a slouched hat, black beard, mysterious cloak, and the boots. After pacing to and fro in much agitation he struck his forehead and burst out in a wild strain, singing of his hatred to Roderigo, his love for Zara, and his pleasing resolution to kill the one and win the other. The gruff tones of Hugo's voice, with an occasional shout when his feelings overcame him, were very impressive, and the audience applauded the moment he paused for breath. Bowing with the air of one accustomed to public praise, he stole to the cavern and ordered Hagar to come forth with a commanding "What ho, minion! I need thee!"

Out came Meg, with gray horse-hair hanging about her face, a red and black robe, a staff, and cabalistic signs upon her cloak. Hugo demanded a potion to make Zara adore

him, and one to destroy Roderigo. Hagar, in a fine dramatic melody, promised both and proceeded to call upon the spirit who would bring the love philter:

Hither, hither, from thy home,
Airy sprite, I bid thee come!
Born of roses, fed on dew,
Charms and potions canst thou brew?
Bring me here, with elfin speed,
The fragrant philter which I need;
Make it sweet and swift and strong,
Spirit, answer now my song!

A soft strain of music sounded, and then at the back of the cave appeared a little figure in cloudy white, with glittering wings, golden hair, and a garland of roses on its head. Waving a wand, it sang:

Hither I come
From my airy home,
Afar in the silver moon.
Take the magic spell,
And use it well,
Or its power will vanish soon!

And dropping a small gilded bottle at the witch's feet, the spirit vanished. Another chant from Hagar produced another apparition—not a lovely one; for with a bang, an ugly black imp appeared, and having croaked a reply, tossed a dark bottle at Hugo and disappeared with a mocking laugh. Having warbled his thanks and put the potions in his boots, Hugo departed; and Hagar informed the audience that as he had killed a few of her friends in times

past she has cursed him, and intends to thwart his plans, and be revenged on him. Then the curtain fell, and the audience reposed and ate candy while discussing the merits of the play.

A good deal of hammering went on before the curtain rose again, but when it became evident what a masterpiece of stage-carpentering had been got up, no one murmured at the delay. It was truly superb! A tower rose to the ceiling; halfway up appeared a window, with a lamp burning at it, and behind the white curtain appeared Zara in a lovely blue and silver dress, waiting for Roderigo. He came in gorgeous array, with plumed cap, red cloak, chestnut lovelocks, a guitar, and the boots, of course. Kneeling at the foot of the tower, he sang a serenade in melting tones. Zara replied and after a musical dialogue consented to fly. Then came the grand effect of the play. Roderigo produced a rope ladder with five steps to it, threw up one end, and invited Zara to descend. Timidly she crept from her lattice, put her hand on Roderigo's shoulder, and was about to leap gracefully down when, "Alas for Zara!" she forgot her train—it caught in the window; the tower tottered, leaned forward, fell with a crash, and buried the unhappy lovers in the ruins!

A universal shriek arose as the russet boots waved wildly from the wreck, and a golden head emerged,

exclaiming, "I told you so! I told you so!" With wonderful presence of mind, Don Pedro, the cruel sire, rushed in, dragged out his daughter, with a hasty aside, "Don't laugh! Act as if it was all right!" and ordering Roderigo up, banished him from the kingdom with wrath and scorn. Though decidedly shaken by the fall of the tower upon him, Roderigo defied the old gentleman and refused to stir. This dauntless example fired Zara: she also defied her sire, and he ordered them both to the deepest dungeons of the castle. A stout little retainer came in with chains and led them away, looking very much frightened, and evidently forgetting the speech he ought to have made.

Act third was the castle hall; and here Hagar appeared, having come to free the lovers and finish off Hugo. She hears him coming and hides; sees him put the potions into two cups of wine and bid the timid little servant "Bear them to the captives in their cells and tell them I shall come anon." The servant takes Hugo aside to tell him something, and Hagar changes the cups for two others which are harmless. Ferdinando, the "minion," carries them away, and Hagar puts back the cup which holds the poison meant for Roderigo. Hugo, getting thirsty after a long warble, drinks it, loses his wits, and after a good deal of clutching and stamping, falls flat and dies, while Hagar informs him what she has done in a song of ex-

quisite power and melody.

This was a truly thrilling scene, though some persons might have thought that the sudden tumbling down of a quantity of long hair rather marred the effect of the villain's death. He was called before the curtain, and with great propriety appeared, leading Hagar, whose singing was considered more wonderful than all the rest of the performance put together.

Act fourth displayed the despairing Roderigo on the point of stabbing himself because he has been told that Zara has deserted him. Just as the dagger is at his heart, a lovely song is sung under his window, informing him that Zara is true but in danger, and he can save her if he will. A key is thrown in, which unlocks the door, and in a spasm of rapture he tears off his chains and rushes away to find and rescue his ladylove.

Act fifth opened with a stormy scene between Zara and Don Pedro. He wishes her to go into a convent but she won't hear of it, and after a touching appeal, is about to faint when Roderigo dashes in and demands her hand. Don Pedro refuses because he is not rich. They shout and gesticulate tremendously but cannot agree, and Roderigo is about to bear away the exhausted Zara when the timid servant enters with a letter and a bag from Hagar, who has mysteriously disappeared. The latter informs the party that she be-

queaths untold wealth to the young pair and an awful doom to Don Pedro if he doesn't make them happy. The bag is opened, and several quarts of tin money shower down upon the stage till it is quite glorified with the glitter. This entirely softens the "stern sire": he consents without a murmur, all join in a joyful chorus, and the curtain falls upon the lovers kneeling to receive Don Pedro's blessing in attitudes of the most romantic grace.

Tumultuous applause followed but received an unexpected check; for the cot-bed, on which the "dress circle" was built, suddenly shut up and extinguished the enthusiastic audience. Roderigo and Don Pedro flew to the rescue, and all were taken out unhurt, though many were speechless with laughter. The excitement had hardly subsided when Hannah appeared, with "Mrs. March's compliments, and would the ladies walk down to supper."

This was a surprise, even to the actors, and when they saw the table, they looked at one another in rapturous amazement. It was like Marmee to get up a little treat for them, but anything so fine as this was unheard-of since the departed days of plenty. There was ice cream—actually two dishes of it, pink and white—and cake and fruit and distracting French bonbons, and in the middle of the table, four great bouquets of hot-house flowers!

It quite took their breath away, and they stared first at the table and then at their mother, who looked as if she enjoyed it immensely.

"Is it fairies?" asked Amy.

"It's Santa Claus," said Beth.

"Mother did it;" and Meg smiled her sweetest, in spite of her gray beard and white eyebrows.

"Aunt March had a good fit and sent the supper," cried Jo, with a sudden inspiration.

"All wrong. Old Mr. Laurence sent it," replied Mrs. March.

"The Laurence boy's grandfather! What in the world put such a thing into his head? We don't know him!" exclaimed Meg.

"Hannah told one of his servants about your breakfast party. He is an odd old gentleman, but that pleased him. He knew my father, years ago; and he sent me a polite note this afternoon, saying he hoped I would allow him to express his friendly feeling toward my children by sending them a few trifles in honor of the day. I could not refuse; and so you have a little feast at night to make up for the bread-and-milk breakfast."

"That boy put it into his head, I know he did! He's a capital fellow, and I wish we could get acquainted. He looks as if he'd like to know us; but he's bashful, and Meg is so prim she won't let me speak to him when we pass," said Jo as the plates went round and the ice began to melt out of sight, with "Ohs!" and "Ahs!" of satisfaction.

"You mean the people who live in the big house next door, don't you?" asked one of the girls. "My mother knows old Mr. Laurence, but says he's very proud and doesn't like to mix with his neighbors. He keeps his grandson shut up when he isn't riding or walking with his tutor, and makes him study very hard. We invited him to our party but he didn't come. Mother says he's very nice, though he never speaks to us girls."

"Our cat ran away once and he brought her back, and we talked over the fence and were getting on capitally—all about cricket, and so on—when he saw Meg coming and walked off. I mean to know him someday; for he needs fun, I'm sure he does," said Jo decidedly.

"I like his manners, and he looks like a little gentleman; so I've no objection to your knowing him if a proper opportunity comes. He brought the flowers himself; and I should have asked him in if I had been sure what was going on up-stairs. He looked so wistful as he went away, hearing the frolic and evidently having none of his own."

"It's a mercy you didn't, Mother!" laughed Jo, looking at her boots. "But we'll have another play sometime that he can see. Perhaps, he'll help act; wouldn't that be jolly?"

"I never had such a fine bouquet before! How pretty it is!" And Meg examined her flowers with great interest.

"They are lovely! But Beth's roses are sweeter to me," said Mrs. March, smelling the half-dead posy in her belt.

Beth nestled up to her and whispered softly, "I wish I could send my bunch to father. I'm afraid he isn't having such a merry Christmas as we are."

CHRISTMAS AT HYDE PARK
BY ELEANOR ROOSEVELT

When our children were young, we spent nearly every Christmas holiday at Hyde Park. We always had a party the afternoon of Christmas Eve for all the families who lived on the place. The presents were piled under the tree, and after everyone had been greeted, my husband would choose the children old enough to distribute gifts and send them around to the guests. My mother-in-law herself always gave out her envelopes with money, and I would give out ours. The cornucopias filled with old-fashioned sugar candies and the peppermint canes hanging on the trees were distributed, too, and then our guests would leave us and enjoy their ice cream, cake, and coffee or milk in another room. Later in the day, when the guests had departed, my husband would begin the reading of *A Christmas Carol*. He never read it through; but he would select parts he thought suitable for the youngest members of the family. Then, after supper, he would read other parts for the older ones.

On Christmas morning, I would get up and close the windows in our room, where all the stockings had been hung on the mantel. The little children would be put into our bed and given their stockings to open. The others would sit around the fire. I tried to see that they all had a glass of orange juice before the opening of stockings really began, but the excitement was so great I was not always successful.

Breakfast was late Christmas morning, and my husband resented having to go to church on Christmas Day and sometimes flatly refused to attend. But I would go with my mother-in-law and such children as she could persuade to accompany us. For the most part, however, the children stayed home. In later years, I went to midnight service on Christmas Eve, and we gave up going to church in the morning.

I remembered the excitement as each child grew old enough to have his own sled and would start out after breakfast to try it on the hill behind the stable. Franklin would go coasting with them, and until the children were nearly grown, he was the only one who ever piloted the bobsled down the hill. Everyone came in for a late lunch, and at dusk we would light the candles on the tree again. Only outdoor presents like sleds and skates were distributed in the morning. The rest were kept for the late-afternoon Christmas tree. Again they were piled under the tree, and my husband and the children scrambled around it, and he called the names.

At first, my mother-in-law did a great deal of shopping and wrapping, and the Hyde Park Christmas always included her gifts. Later, she

found shopping too difficult. Then she would give each person a check, though she managed very often to give her son the two things she knew he would not buy for himself—silk shirts and silk pajamas. These she bought in London, as a rule, and saved for his Christmas, which to her was always very special.

In the early years of our marriage, I did a great deal more sewing and embroidering than I've done since, so many of my gifts were things I had made. The family still has a few pieces of Italian cutwork embroidery and other kinds of my perfectly useless handwork. I look back, however, with some pleasure on the early Hyde Park days, when I would have a table filled with pieces of silk and make sachets of different scents. I would dry pine needles at Campobello Island and make them into sweet-smelling bags for Christmas. Now I rarely give a present I have made, and perhaps, it is just as well, for what one buys is likely to be better made!

Each of the children had a special preference in gifts. When Anna was a small child, her favorite present was a rocking horse, on which she spent many hours. Later, she was to spend even more hours training her own horse, which her great-uncle Mr. Warren Delano gave her. One of the nicest gifts we could possibly give her as she grew older was something for her horse, Natomah. Jimmy loved boats from the very beginning, whether he floated them

in the bathtub or later competed with his father in the regattas of toy boats on the Hudson River. Elliott was always trying to catch up with his older brother and sister; but because he was delicate as a child, I think he read more than the others. I remember that books and games were very acceptable gifts for him. Franklin, Jr., and John were a pair and had to have pretty much the same things, or they would quarrel over them. They had learned together to ride and to swim, so gifts for outdoor sports were always favorites of theirs.

My children teased me because their stockings inevitably contained toothbrushes, toothpaste, nail cleaners, soap, washcloths, etc. They said Mother never ceased to remind them that cleanliness was next to godliness—even on Christmas morning. In the toe of each stocking, I always put a purse, with a dollar bill for the young ones and a five-dollar bill for the older ones. These bills were hoarded to supplement the rather meager allowances they had. When I was able to buy sucre d'orge (barley sugar), I put that in their stockings, together with some old-fashioned peppermint sticks; but as they grew older, this confection seemed to vanish from the market, and I had to give it up and substitute chocolates. The stockings also contained families of little china pigs or rabbits or horses, which the children placed on their bookshelves.

The children themselves could

probably tell much better than I can the things they remember most about these years. But I know that all of them have carried on many of the Hyde Park Christmas traditions with their children. Today, some of my grandchildren are establishing the same customs, and my great-grandchildren will one day remember the same kind of Christmas we started so many years ago.

BIZCOCHITOS

These anise-cinnamon cookies are traditional among the Pueblo Indians of Taos, New Mexico, and today are enjoyed throughout the state.

1 pound shortening
2 cups sugar
2 eggs
2 teaspoons anise seed
3 teaspoons baking powder

6 cups flour
1 teaspoon salt
6 ounces sweet wine
1 teaspoon cinnamon

Cream the shortening and blend in all but ½ cup of the sugar. Add the eggs and anise. Sift together the remaining dry ingredients; add to the shortening mixture gradually, alternating with the wine and ending with the flour.

Lightly flour a pastry board and roll out the dough into a thin sheet. Cut with cookie cutter and sprinkle with ½ cup of sugar and cinnamon. Bake in a preheated 350-degree oven till lightly browned, about 10 minutes.

ROAST TURKEY WITH CORNBREAD STUFFING

8   tablespoons butter
1   large onion, chopped
2   large Granny Smith apples, cored
     and coarsely chopped
¾   pound sausage meat
6   cups crumbled stale cornbread
1½   teaspoons sage

salt and freshly ground pepper to taste
2 large sprigs parsley, chopped
1 cup raisins
1 cup walnut halves
20 pound turkey
butter for basting

Melt the 8 tablespoons butter and sauté the onion until soft, about 20 minutes. Transfer to a large mixing bowl and set aside. Over medium heat, brown crumbled sausage meat, stirring. Transfer to mixing bowl with slotted spoon. Cook the apples in the rendered fat until slightly softened. Transfer with slotted spoon to mixing bowl. Add remaining ingredients and mix well.

Stuff and truss the turkey. Place in a lightly greased roasting pan and dot with butter. Set in the middle of a preheated 450-degree oven and reduce heat at once to 350 degrees. Roast, basting frequently, allowing about 15 to 20 minutes per pound. (A meat thermometer set in the thickest part of the bird should register 180 to 185 degrees.)

CRANBERRY SAUCE

2 cups water
2 cups sugar
1 pound cranberries, washed

1   teaspoon grated orange rind
½ cup orange juice or Grand Marnier

In a saucepan dissolve the sugar in the water, stirring. Bring to a boil and cook for five minutes. Add the berries and simmer, stirring, for another five minutes or so, until ber-

ries have become translucent and started to pop. Add rind and juice or Grand Marnier, pour into a serving bowl, and chill until set.

CANDIED YAMS

4   medium yams
salt to taste
½ cup brown sugar

¼ teaspoon ginger
2   tablespoons butter
8   large marshmallows (optional)

Cook yams, with skins, in boiling water to cover till just about tender but not mushy. Peel and cut in halves; arrange in ovenproof casserole. Sprinkle with salt, sugar, and ginger; dot with butter and top with marshmallows, if desired. Bake in a preheated 375-degree oven for 25 minutes, or until sugar has glazed the yams.

SERVES SIX TO EIGHT

COLONIAL EGGNOG

10 egg yolks
½ pound confectioner's sugar
2   pints whiskey

3 cups milk
1 pint heavy whipping cream
freshly grated nutmeg

Beat the egg yolks till fluffy, then beat in sugar. Gradually add the whiskey, beating; add milk and chill. Immediately before serving whip the cream and fold in gently. Top with a dusting of grated nutmeg.

MAKES 20 SERVINGS

HOT BUTTERED RUM

This bracing cup has warmed many a New England Christmas.

2 ounces dark rum
twist of lemon peel
stick cinnamon

8 ounces cider (hard or not, according
    to taste) or 8 ounces water, boiling

Put rum, lemon peel, and cinnamon in a large mug or tankard; add cider or water; stir with cinnamon stick.

MAKES ONE TEN-OUNCE SERVING

SELECTED BIBLIOGRAPHY

Banta, N. Moore. *St. Nicholas Christmas Book* (Chicago: A. Flanagan Company, 1925).

Becker, Mary Lamberton, ed. *The Home Book of Christmas* (New York: Dodd, Mead & Company, 1941).

Bishop, Claire Huchet. *Happy Christmas!* (New York: Stephen Daye Press, 1956).

Boutell, Zelta. *The Christmas Cookbook* (New York: The Viking Press, 1953).

Brady, Agnes Maria. *Christmastide* (Dallas: Banks Upshaw and Company, 1937).

Cagner, Ewert. *Swedish Christmas* (Gottenburg: Tre Tryckare, 1954).

Centuries Ago: Songs of Bethlehem (New York: Anson D.F. Randolph Company, 1884).

Christmas, Frederick Ernest. *A Christmas Anthology* (London: The St. Hugh's Press Limited, 1934).

Coffin, Tristram P. *The Book of Christmas Folklore* (New York: The Seabury Press, 1973).

Crippen, T.G. *Christmas and Christmas Lore* (London: Blackie and Son Limited, 1923).

Dawson, W.F. *Christmas: Its Origins and Associations* (London: Elliot Stock, 1902).

Eaton, Anne Thaxter. *The Animal's Christmas* (New York: The Viking Press, 1944).

Epperson, Kathleen. *The Christmas Cookbook* (San Francisco: Nitty Gritty Productions, 1969).

Foley, Daniel J. *Christmas The World Over* (New York and Philadelphia: Chilton, 1963).

Gates, Philip, ed. *Christmas in Song and Story* (New York: Cockcroft & Company, 1876).

Haugan, Randolph E., ed. *Christmas* (an annual magazine) (Minneapolis: Augsburg Publishing House, 1931–1936).

Hervey, Thomas K. *The Book of Christmas* (Boston: Roberts Brothers, 1888).

A Holiday Book for Christmas and the New Year (London: Ingram, Cook and Company, 1852).

Ickis, Marguerite. *The Book of Christmas* (New York: Dodd, Mead & Company, 1960).

The Life Book of Christmas, volumes I–III (New York: Time Incorporated, 1963).

Lohan, Robert and Maria, eds. *A New Christmas Treasury* (New York: Stephen Daye Press, 1954).

Morris, Harrison S., ed. *In the Yule-Log Glow* (Philadelphia: J.B. Lippincott Company, 1891).

Pasley, Virginia. *The Christmas Cookie Book* (Boston: Little, Brown and Company, 1949).

Pearson, N.F. *The Stories of Our Christmas Customs* (Loughborough: Willis & Hepworth Ltd, 1964).

Posselt, Eric. *The World's Greatest Christmas Stories* (New York: Ziff-Davis, 1949).

Pringle, Mary P. and Clara A. Urann. *Yule-Tide in Many Lands* (Boston: Lothrop, Lee & Shepard Company, 1916).

Roosevelt, Eleanor. *Eleanor Roosevelt's Christmas Book* (New York: Dodd, Mead & Company, 1963).

Sayre, Eleanor. *A Christmas Book* (New York: Clarkson N. Potter, Inc., 1966).

Schauffler, Robert Haven, ed. *Christmas* (New York: Moffat, Yard & Company, 1907).

Sciutto, Gretta McOmber and Margaret Egbert Thompson. *In the Very Name of Christmas* (Boston: Chapman & Grimes, Inc., 1951).

Scott, Temple. *The Christmas Treasury of Song and Verse* (New York: The Baker & Taylor Company, 1910).

Smith, Elva S. and Alice Isabel Hazeltine. *The Christmas Book of Legends and Stories* (New York: Lothrop, Lee & Shepard Company, 1944).

Spicer, Dorothy Gladys. *46 Days of Christmas* (New York: Coward-McCann, Inc., 1968).

Wernecke, Herbert H., ed. *Celebrating Christmas Around the World* (Philadelphia: The Westminster Press, 1968).

—*Christmas Customs Around the World* (Philadelphia: The Westminster Press, 1959).

—*Christmas Stories from Many Lands* (Philadelphia: The Westminster Press, 1961).

—*Tales of Christmas From Near and Far* (Philadelphia: The Westminster Press, 1963).